Business Management for the Professional Photographer

Business Management for the Professional Photographer

Sy Gutterman

Amphoto
American Photographic
Book Publishing Co., Inc.

NEW YORK, NEW YORK

 Published in New York,
New York, by American Photographic Book Publishing Co., Inc.

Library of Congress Cataloging in Publication Data
Gutterman, Sy.
Business management for the professional photographer.
Includes index.
1. Photography–Business methods. I. Title.

TR581.G83 770'.68 79-26992

ISBN 0-8174-3568-9 (hardbound)

Manufactured in the United States of America

10 9 8 7 6 5 4 3 2 1

Table of Contents

Preface 7

Chapter 1 Business Structure 9

Chapter 2 The Business Contract 11

Chapter 3 A Business Contract for the Professional Photographer 20

Chapter 4 The Filing System 31

Chapter 5 Proof-Negative Index 38

Chapter 6 Order Forms 46

Chapter 7 Album Tabulation Form 53

Chapter 8 Permissions, Disclaimers, and Information Forms 60

Chapter 9 Accounting and Bookkeeping 79

Chapter 10 Studios and Leases 98

Chapter 11 The Professional Photographer 105

Chapter 12 Personnel 107

Chapter 13 Communications 115

Chapter 14 Customer Relations 117

Chapter 15 Education 120

Chapter 16 Equipment 123

Chapter 17 Your Processing Lab 126

Chapter 18 Pricing 129

Chapter 19 The Profit Picture 133

Chapter 20 Sales and Marketing 136

Chapter 21 Collections 149

Chapter 22 The Business of Photography 152

Chapter 23 Buying and Selling a Business 155

Closing Comment 158

Index 159

Preface

The bottom line of any business operation is profits and losses. In order to remain solvent, every business must show a profit. Whether operated on an item-for-item exchange, or barter basis, or on the exchange of money for services rendered, the bottom line is always the same.

Although many books have been written on general business operations, very few have covered the business of photography and even fewer have ventured to treat photography as a total enterprise.

This book will approach photography as a business, not as an art. The main purpose will be to help the professional photographer organize his operation into an efficient machine, thereby cutting operating costs and transferring those funds to the profit side of the ledger, instead.

CHAPTER 1 Business Structure

There are three basic types of business structure: individual ownership, partnership, and corporation. An individually owned business may be a small one, or it may be a large company. While the individual owner has great flexibility in controlling the entire business operation, he is also responsible for all the debts incurred. If the business fails, the individual's personal assets can be seized to satisfy those debts.

Partnerships can be equal or unequal. Equal partners share equally in the profits and in the losses. Unequal partners divide the profits and the losses according to the percentage of the business owned by each one. While we usually think of partnerships as a two-person operation, there may be any number of partners. In a general partnership, all the partners are liable for the debts incurred by the business: Each partner may have his personal assets seized in order to satsify those debts. This is not unlike individual ownership.

Partnerships should be very carefully considered. In those states that have community-property laws the partners may find they have an unwanted addition to the partnership: the divorced mate of one of the partners.

A corporation is a group of people who have been granted a charter by a state agency to operate a business enterprise. The corporation may consist of a president, secretary, board of directors, and stockholders, plus other elements of corporate structure required by the laws governing corporations in the individual state in which the corporation is formed. Corporations can buy and sell other corporations, individually owned businesses, and partnerships, although all such acquisitions or disposals must be approved by the stockholders.

Creditors can file claims against a corporation, but their limits of seizure are against the assets of the corporation and not against the individual assets of the individuals in the corporation.

There are many items to be considered *before* a business is set up as an individually owned entity, a partnership, or a corporation. There are different types of partnerships and of corporations, such as, limited or unlimited, and each has its purpose. Only an accountant and an attorney can advise a person, or persons, as to the best choice of business structure.

CHAPTER 2

The Business Contract

Contracts are the basis for all business commitments. Contracts can be in the form of a written document, a verbal agreement, a handshake, or any combination of the three. Centuries ago, when most business transactions were made on a personal basis, simplicity was the accepted rule. Today the world has shrunk because of technological advancements; virtually all our movements are controlled, scanned, or registered by electronics, and contracts are most often complex documents. A working knowledge of contracts is therefore desirable.

Although a word and a handshake may still be acceptable to some persons, the universal business agreement is a written contract. This may be in the form of a Purchase Order (P.O.), a Work Order (W.O.), or an actual business contract.

People are generally wary of lengthy contracts and of documents containing small, or fine, print on the bottom of the page or on the back of the sheet. There are several reasons why many of the contracts we are asked to sign do contain fine print. A legitimate one is that without fine print many contracts would occupy a lot of space on paper, sometimes making the documents unwieldy. On the other hand, small print is sometimes used to confuse the reader, to have him skip over the wording and sign the document without fully understanding what he is agreeing to. The truth is that most persons do not fully read every document they sign.

The Photography Business Contract

If the contract is the basic operating tool of the business world, then it is so for the photographer's business, as well. No job should be undertaken without a suitable contract. The big question is: What is a suitable contract?

The basic contract. A suitable contract is one that will fully protect the photographer in almost every contingency. *Almost* is said for good reason. No matter how ironclad a contract or agreement may be, there will be someone who can devise a method of circumventing it. So you, the business person, must do what other business people do: Make your contract as protective as possible. Make it protective to the point where your client will not want to contest the contract in a court of law unless the client is absolutely certain of being victorious.

In other words, you are not out to cheat your customers. You are going to give them a product or service for the monies paid to you. You are going to tell them, in writing, exactly what they are going to receive, what they are expected to do in their relationship with you, and, of equal importance, what your responsibilities to them are.

A very basic contract will show that the customer will pay X amount of dollars for Y amount of photographs or photographic services. To state everything in one simple sentence would be very convenient. But then the modifiers come into play. Modifiers are the "terms and conditions" we so often see in contractual agreements.

Terms and conditions. Let us see how modifiers affect the basic agreement. What will you charge for 40 photographs instead of the "usual' 24? What do you charge for traveling 30 miles to the job, instead of the alloted 5 miles? Do you differentiate between the types of albums or frames offered, if these are part of the job? Or are they all priced the same? How much are extra photographs purchased after the original order has been delivered? Are you the photographer who will do the work? How long can the customer keep the proofs? Who do the proofs belong to? What if the customer does not return some, or all, proofs? What if the customer does not like the color of the delivered photographs? What happens if there is a failure of equipment and the photographs do not turn out? What happens if . . . ? This phrase is the key to the basic need for a document to protect the photographer.

What Happens If?

There are documented cases on record of lawsuits that were begun against photographers and decided for the plaintiffs. An item in *The Cleveland* (Ohio) *Press* on Tuesday, September 9, 1975, stated that the photography studio agreed to a $5000 settlement *(Seidler v. Nelson's Photography Studio of Lyndhurst).* According to the article, "Common Pleas Judge August Pryatel said the studio lawyer admitted that the photographer's camera jammed and that many negatives were blank."

How many photographers can truthfully say they have never experienced some malfunction that resulted in blank negatives? How did you explain the absence of those photographs? "The lab lost the film" is an often-heard excuse. Another one frequently used is, "The films were lost in the mails." Granted that those incidents do happen, how does the photographer protect himself against a lawsuit in such circumstances? After all, if guests flew from Chicago to New York for a wedding, and the photographs of them at the event were lost, how are you going to restage the shots? What if aged Uncle Bill went to his heavenly repose shortly after the wedding?

How many cameras, similar to that famous workhorse the Rolleiflex, or "Rollei," have had the flash-synchronization lever permanently locked in strobe position? Photographers have done this to prevent the lever from being accidentally reset to the flash-bulb position. We all know that this type of sync "failure" will result in lost photographs unless the shutter speed happens to be set around one-half second, the camera is held perfectly still throughout the slow movement of the shutter blades, and there is sufficient ambient light to put a usable image on the film.

With wedding photographers usually shooting at 1/125 or 1/250 sec., you can safely say that off-sync will result in no photograph. That being a very good possibility, what would happen if the photographer shot the entire wedding with the incorrect sync setting? The duties were performed in good faith. By usual operations, a usable set of photographs should result. Then, when the camera is being stowed in an equipment bag after the event, the sync lever is found to be in the wrong position. The photographer's heart sinks. Was it like that for all the shots, or part of them, or was it pushed over at just that moment? The photographer leaves the event with the unhappy knowledge that he or she may wind up with a total blank, a partial blank, or perhaps a good set of negatives. All one can do is sweat it out until the film comes back from the lab.

Although sync failures are probably the most common malfunctions experienced in shooting, there are others involving internal camera malfunctions. Let us also not forget that labs do lose or damage films and that material does get lost in the mails. The basic fact is that the contracting photographer or studio is liable for damages.

Let us consider fashion photography. What would be the unhappy result if the photographer experienced equipment failure while on location and didn't know about it until the return to the studio, or after development of the film? Besides losing the money specified for doing the work, how much can the photographer be sued for? Without adaquate protection by an effective contract, it would be a safe guess to say "the sky's the limit."

Bear in mind that a photographer protected by a good contract must still operate on the premise that there is no protection. That means the contract should not be given as an excuse for slovenly work, for using equipment that is not serviced regularly and is not dependable, or for not taking maximum precautions in the handling of film and photographs. The contract must be used as a last-resort protection device, not as a license for neglect or carelessness.

Alternative Forms of Agreement

Many photographers say they use a *condition-of-sale* statement as a contract. Several lines on a 5″ × 8″ sales receipt is a poor excuse for a contract. Many processing labs have found that the disclaimer notice, so widely acclaimed as a protection device for many years, has been ruled invalid in some instances. And a few lines on a sales receipt is nothing better than a disclaimer notice.

A survey of business contracts being used by professional photographers indicates that some of the documents attempt to convey the impression of being a legal instrument. Some contracts may have the emblem of the Professional Photographers of America,

Inc. (P.P. of A.), or of local or state photography associations. Members of these organizations have the privilege of using the group's official emblems, and they can use them on documents without prior approval by the organization. The emblem reinforces the "professional" impression that is desired. But use of these documents that only look legal and binding may be detrimental to the party that needs the protection: the photographer. This printed "nothingness" can prevent collection of accounts receivable and may even cause the photographer to become the victim of a lawsuit.

A Tested Contract Form

The contract outlined in the next chapter is a revised version of the *New Horizons Photography* contract published in the January 1976 issue of *Studio Photography* magazine. At that time it had been in use for several years and had been tested in court. One court case involved a client who had contracted for commercial photographs of an industrial plant. Two photographers worked several days on location and the studio delivered the proofs, as called for in the contract. Instead of ordering enlargements as specified in the contract, however, the company used the proofs to accomplish their purpose.

After many weeks of frustration the studio took the case to small-claims court. The studio wanted to either complete the order as contracted or receive the full dollar amount specified in the contract.

When the case came to court, the commissioner asked for a copy of the contract. After hearing both sides of the case he questioned the defendant. He wanted to know why the company did not want to order the enlargements stipulated in the contract. The defendant admitted that the reason for having photographs made was to obtain additional financing for his company; that the proofs had accomplished the purpose; and that therefore there was no need for the enlargements.

Justice was swift. The commissioner ruled that the studio was to be paid the full amount specified in the contract. The studio did not have to supply any of the enlargements, and the defendant could retain the proofs. The commissioner said the studio was willing to act in good faith and complete the contract, and that it was not the studio's fault that the company had utilized the proofs for their purpose.

The commissioner asked the studio owner about the contract form. He said he had never seen as comprehensive a contract for use by photographers. He asked for a copy for his reference file.

In another situation, movies of a wedding were ordered at the same time as an album of still photographs. The client wanted the movies delivered within one week after the wedding. In return, the studio wanted the full dollar amount of the contract prior to delivery of the motion-picture film. The reason was simple: The bridegroom was employed by a film-processing lab. It would be a simple matter to print stills from the film—and neglect to call for the rest of the contract: the album of prints. After several telephone discussions the client called with the final solution. He had conferred with his attorney and received these words of advice: "You *may* be able to crawl out from under this contract, but you would have to crawl mighty low in order to do it. Pay the man, conduct the rest of your business openly and according to the agreement, and don't bother me. My costs outweigh anything you might hope to gain with your stubbornness." The ironic outcome was that the two principals became friends.

Beware of "gremlins." The first revision to the original version of this contract came into being with the sudden discovery that "gremlins" were wreaking havoc with color photographs: Tan garments were turning purple in the final prints, green showed as muddy brown, and black was not always black. Clients complained; photographers were stunned. The processing laboratores said they were not playing tricks; that as long as facial tones were correct the other colors were supposedly correct. "Supposedly correct" didn't help the photographer. Then other mysterious things started to appear: Some women's faces looked ghostly on the print, persons had specks on their otherwise-well-groomed hair, and women's lips sometimes appeared white.

The Eastman Kodak Company came to the rescue, explaining this phenomenon as *anomalous reflectance.* One definition for "anomalous" is "abnormal." Basically, what the film saw was not what our eyes perceived. Our eyes did not see as broad a color spectrum as the film did. The synthetic dyes of the products were in a range of the spectrum that was beyond the capabilities of our eyes but within that covered by present-day color films. Therefore, the cloth may have appeared tan to the human eye, but it photographed in its true color, purple. Hair sprays were responsible for the specks on people's heads, and the ingredients in cosmetics were the culprits for the sometimes ghostly facial appearances.

While the true colors would not be seen by the human eye under normal lighting conditions, they could be seen under "black light"–ultraviolet radiation. Carrying a portable UV lamp around would be bothersome, at best. Exposing the principals of an event to the UV scrutiny would be tedious and could meet with opposition from everyone involved. The best solution was a halfway measure, to explain anomalous reflectance to clients and offer to test clothes and cosmetics prior to the event. But what about the final photographs? What if there were still some fluorescence? What could you, the photographer, do about it, and what was your liability?

There isn't much you can really do with fluorescent materials except call for airbrushing or spotting with dyes. A medium would have to be reached between facial tones and garment colors in the printing process. After that, the clothes either have to remain as printed or be color-corrected by hand. This is a costly procedure, to say the least. Why should the photographer be blamed for something that is beyond his control? Why should the photographer be expected to pay for color correction when the error is not due to any negligence on his part or on the part of the processing lab? A good, effective, contract will contain a clause for this contingency.

Time charges and cancellations. Another item to consider in contracts is the time spent with a client. Many photographers who operate out of their homes may go to the client's home or place of business instead of having the client come to the photographer's place of business. Traveling is not only time consuming but also costs money. Any time you move your car costs money. Let us assume that you do get a job by going to a client's home. Let us also assume that there is a consumer-protection law in your state to the effect that the client has 72 hours during which he can cancel a contract signed at some place other than the vendor's place of business and that all monies paid as deposit must be refunded upon written demand. If you have spent one or two hours closing the sale, plus travel time, who is going to reimburse you if the job is canceled? Many shoppers-at-home like to do a lot of comparison shopping. There is nothing to stop them from placing deposits with more than one photographer and then choosing one and asking the others for refunds. The shoppers are protected by the law, and their money must be refunded. A good contract will contain a cancellation clause to protect the merchant—the photographer, in this case.

Why a cancellation clause? What's wrong with keeping deposits? Well, in the first place, under the law cited, deposits must be refunded in full. No mention is made of cancellation fees. But cancellation fees could be used to cover the expenses and time used in traveling to and from the client's residence or place of business and for the time spent in setting up the preliminary paperwork. With a cancellation fee, the habitual "shopping" shopper would curtail a lot of the home activity usually carried on at the merchant's expense.

Protecting the client. What about the client? Doesn't the customer warrant protection? Most assuredly. The contract explained in detail in the next chapter contains clauses that protect the customer against several things, including malfunction of equipment and delays in delivery when there are no extraordinary circumstances involved. There is absolutely no reason for a couple to wait six months or more after they turn in their order for their album of wedding photographs. This type of operation is prevalent in many large cities on the eastern seaboard and is indicative of the disregard some business persons have for captive clients. There is no valid excuse these merchants can offer to vindicate this way of doing business. Service *after* sales is an important company product.

What Is a Contract?

Every document you sign is, in effect, a contract of sorts. When you park your car in a pay parking lot, read the ticket that is given to you. It is an agreement, and an agreement is a contract. When you purchase items on a charge account, there is an agreement in effect about the ownership of those items until they are paid for in full. That is a contract. When you get married, you sign a marriage contract. When you ask someone to maintain the lawn at your residence, that is a contract. Any agreement is a contract. Why not make your business contract work for you?

A Business Contract for the Professional Photographer

CHAPTER 3

A business contract should be long enough to protect both buyer and seller but not long enough to become a volume. What we have in the New Horizons Photography business contract is a *protection* document. Because a client may resist a lengthy contract, it is a good idea to talk briefly before filling in one word on paper.

"Mrs. Jones," you might say, "this is our standard all-inclusive contract. We use it for all our business. Many of the listed items will not apply to you, and we will mark them N/A—'not applicable.' We will discuss the contract together. After you are certain you understand it, and you sign it, you will receive a copy of it."

A short talk like that, plus sales personality, will get you over the first hurdle.

Let us consider the contract item by item.

How to Write the Contract

The contract number is filled in on the first line. This number then becomes the basic key number for the entire job. Every item associated with this assignment will carry this job number. (Another chapter will explain how the contract number, or job number, is used for negative, print, and album identification.)

THE ABOVE-NAMED STUDIO IS HEREBY ENGAGED TO PROVIDE THE ______________ . . .

Here the type of photography is inserted: Wedding, Bar Mitzvah, Commercial, Legal, Industrial, Portrait, etc.

FOR ______________ . . . .

The client's name is inserted.

ON <u>(day of week)</u> THE <u>(date)</u> OF <u>(month, year)</u>.

Write in the day(s) the photography is to be done.

Item 1A denotes the type of sitting for formal portraits, and the time and date. Prices should be noted.

Item 1B tells where the formal portraits are to be taken: in the studio, on location, or both.

Item 1C designates the type of photographic medium. The number of photographs should be entered on this line, together with price.

Item 1D is a catchall line where slide shows or recorded tapes can be entered.

Item 2 is used in photographic assignments other than weddings, bar mitzvahs, and portrait sittings. Commercial, legal, editorial, and industrial photography are a few of the classifications that would be listed here. (A long list can "overflow" to Item 6.)

Item 3 is self-explanatory. All albums, together with applicable prices, are entered here.

Items 4 and 5 usually work together, as the note just below implies. ***Item 4*** can be used for special coverage of guests, where specific persons or groups are to be photographed. Then, at a wedding or bar mitzvah the client may ask that all the guests seated at tables be photographed (***Item 5***). Arrangement of the individual groups at each table is a physical job that is multiplied by the number of tables. It also causes additional expenditures in materials and lab fees. These added expenses must be borne by the client who requests the service. A photographer cannot be expected to photograph 10, 15, or 20 tables and then have those photographs rejected from the total picture count in the basic order. This is noted in the comment marked by the asterisk (*).

Item 6 is another catchall clause. It can be used for any kind of photographic assignment. It can also be used as an "overflow" space for any of the other items (such as Item 2 or Item 7).

Item 7 states that a specific amount of time will be spent on the job, and that overtime will be charged at specified rates for excess time on the job.

Item 8 is self-explanatory. Studio personnel must be allowed time off for meals or provided with food if the total working time exceeds the specified four hours. At most receptions and party events there are extra provisions, and the caterers, if instructed by the host, are usually willing to serve photographers and musicians at no additional charge if there is an overabundance of food.

Item 9 states when the photographer will start.

CONTRACT NO.____________

THE ABOVE NAMED STUDIO IS HEREBY ENGAGED TO PROVIDE THE ____________

FOR ____________

ON ________ THE ________ OF ________ 19 ____

THE FOLLOWING SERVICES ARE CONTRACTED FOR:

		COL. 1	COL. 2 NO TAX
(1A)	☐ FORMAL PORTRAITS DATE ________ TIME ________ AM PM TYPE OF SITTING ________		
(1B)	☐ STUDIO ☐ ON LOCATION ________		
(1C)	☐ CANDIDS ☐ COLOR PRINTS ☐ COLOR TRANSPARENCIES ☐ COLOR MOVIES ☐ BLACK AND WHITE ________		
(1D)	☐ OTHER ________		
(2)	HOURLY RATE ________		
(3)	ALBUM(S): STYLE/TYPE: ________		
(4)	*OTHER COVERAGE/ADDITIONAL SERVICE(S): ________		
(5)	*TABLE COVERAGE: ________		
	*IF SPECIFIC PERSONS AND/OR TABLE GROUPS ARE TO BE PHOTOGRAPHED, THESE PHOTOGRAPHS MUST BE TAKEN AS PART OF THE BASIC ORDER. THIS CONDITION ALSO APPLIES TO ANY SERVICE(S) NOTED IN ITEM #4.		
(6)	________ PHOTOGRAPHY AS FOLLOWS ________		
	SUB TOTAL		
	SALES TAX		
	COL. 1 + COL. 2		
	TOTAL AMT		

(7) TOTAL TIME ALLOTTED FOR THIS JOB IS______HOURS. TIME IN EXCESS WILL BE CONSIDERED OVERTIME AND CHARGED FOR AT THE FOLLOWING RATE(S)

$______ PER HOUR OR FRACTION THEREOF FOR EACH PHOTOGRAPHER

$______ PER HOUR OR FRACTION THEREOF FOR EACH ASSISTANT PHOTOGRAPHER

OVERTIME FEES ARE DUE AND PAYABLE IMMEDIATELY UPON COMPLETION OF THE EVENT.

(8) IF THE TOTAL ELAPSED JOB/LOCATION TIME EXCEEDS FOUR (4) HOURS, ALL STUDIO PERSONNEL MUST EITHER BE SUPPLIED FOOD AND NON-ALCOHOLIC BEVERAGE(S) BY THE CUSTOMER, OR THESE ITEMS MADE AVAILABLE TO THEM TOGETHER WITH A TIME PERIOD OF ONE-HALF (1/2) HOUR OF OFF TIME FOR THE PURPOSE OF EATING THESE ITEMS.

(9) THE PHOTOGRAPHER(S) WILL START AT APPROXIMATELY ______ A. M. ______ P. M.

(10) ______ PHOTOGRAPHER(S) WILL BE ASSIGNED TO THIS JOB ACCORDING TO THE FOLLOWING SCHEDULE OR AS DETERMINED BY THE STUDIO:

UP TO _____ PEOPLE _____ PHOTOGRAPHER(S), _____ ASSISTANT PHOTOGRAPHER(S)

OVER _____ PEOPLE _____ PHOTOGRAPHER(S), _____ ASSISTANT PHOTOGRAPHER(S)

FOR MOVIES AND TRANSPARENCIES, ADDITIONAL ARRANGEMENTS WILL BE MADE. SEE ITEM #6.

(11) IT IS AGREED THAT THE STUDIO CAN NOT GUARANTEE THAT ANY ONE PARTICULAR PERSON OR PERSONS WILL PERFORM THE DUTIES/SERVICES AS SPECIFIED IN THIS CONTRACT, AND THAT THE STUDIO HAS THE RIGHT TO ASSIGN ANY PHOTOGRAPHER(S) FOR THESE DUTIES/SERVICES.

(12) IT IS UNDERSTOOD THAT THE STUDIO IS THE EXCLUSIVE OFFICIAL PHOTOGRAPHER AND THAT NO PHOTOGRAPH(S) MAY BE TAKEN BY ANY OTHER PHOTOGRAPHER(S) OR PERSON(S) UNLESS WRITTEN PERMISSION IS GRANTED BY THE STUDIO.

(13) THE STUDIO IS NOT BOUND UNTIL THE REQUIRED DEPOSIT OF $______ IS PAID AND RECEIPTED. ADDITIONAL PAYMENTS ARE REQUIRED (AND ARE TO BE MADE) AS FOLLOWS:

$______ ON OR BEFORE ________ ; $______ ON OR BEFORE ________

ADDITIONAL ORDERS MUST BE PAID IN FULL UPON PLACEMENT OF THE ORDER. NO C. O. D. OR BALANCES DUE.

(14) DEPOSITS AND OTHER MONIES PAID HEREUNDER ARE NOT APPLICABLE TO PRODUCTS OR SERVICES OTHER THAN AS SPECIFIED HEREIN.
A CANCELLATION FEE OF ________
SHALL BE DUE AND IMMEDIATELY PAYABLE TO THE STUDIO IN THE EVENT OF CANCELLATION OF THIS CONTRACT BY THE PURCHASER OR REPRESENTATIVE.

(15) THE STUDIO IS NOT LIABLE IN THE EVENT THAT PICTURES CAN NOT BE TAKEN, OR THE STUDIO DOES NOT OR CAN NOT DELIVER PROOFS/APPROVAL PHOTOGRAPHS/PREVIEWS/FINISHED PHOTOGRAPHS, TRANSPARENCIES, MOVIES, OR OTHER CONTRACTED PRODUCTS AND/OR SERVICES DUE TO CIRCUMSTANCES BEYOND THE CONTROL OF THE STUDIO AND/OR ANY OF ITS EMPLOYEES OR REPRESENTATIVES, OR DUE TO MALFUNCTION OF EQUIPMENT — IN WHICH EVENT ALL DEPOSITS WILL BE REFUNDED TO THE PURCHASER OR AUTHORIZED REPRESENTATIVE.

contract can be a protection for both the photographer and the client.

CONTRACT NO. ________________ PAGE 2

(16) IN THE EVENT THE PHOTOGRAPHER IN CHARGE CEASES OPERATION ON THE JOB DUE TO INTERFERENCE(S), OR OTHER FACTOR(S) THAT HE DECIDES MAY BE DETRIMENTAL TO THE PERFORMANCE OF ASSIGNED DUTIES OR TO PERSONAL SAFETY, ALL SUMS ARE DUE AND PAYABLE IMMEDIATELY. ALL SUMS PAID ARE NOT REFUNDABLE NOR CAN THEY BE CREDITED TO ANY OTHER WORK. TERMINATION WITHOUT COMPLETION OF THE ASSIGNED SCHEDULE PRECLUDES DELIVERY OF THE CONTRACTED SERVICE(S) AND/OR PRODUCT(S). PRIOR TO TERMINATION OF ACTIVITY UNDER THIS CLAUSE, THE PHOTOGRAPHER WILL ATTEMPT TO CONTACT THE PURCHASER OR REPRESENTATIVE SO THAT THE PURCHASER OR REPRESENTATIVE MAY EXERT EFFORTS TO CORRECT THE SITUATION.

(17) COLORS MAY NOT REPRODUCE ON PHOTOGRAPHIC MATERIALS THE SAME AS THEY APPEAR TO THE HUMAN EYE. THERE ARE MANY REASONS FOR THIS DISPARITY, AMONG WHICH ARE THE CHEMICALS, DYES, AND MATERIALS USED IN THE MANUFACTURE OF FABRICS, COSMETICS, HAIR SPRAYS AND PREPARATIONS, FOOD COLORING, AND OTHER ITEMS. THE ABILITY TO DISTINGUISH COLORS MAY BE DIFFERENT IN PHOTOGRAPHIC MATERIALS THAN SAID ABILITY IN THE HUMAN EYE.

THE PHOTOGRAPHER/STUDIO HAS NO CONTROL OVER COLOR REPRESENTATIONS AND REPRODUCTIONS DUE TO THE STATED CIRCUMSTANCES AND OTHER CIRCUMSTANCES BEYOND CONTROL OF SAID PHOTOGRAPHER/STUDIO, AND ASSUMES NO RESPONSIBILITY FOR SAME. THE PURCHASER/REPRESENTATIVE AGREES TO PAY ALL COSTS INVOLVED FOR COLOR CORRECTIVE PROCEDURES, IF SUCH WORK IS REQUESTED BY SAID PARTY. IT IS ADDITIONALLY AGREED THAT THERE CAN NOT BE ANY GUARANTEE THAT THE FINAL CORRECTED WORK WILL MATCH THE COLOR(S) AS SEEN BY THE HUMAN EYE, NOR THAT ANY COLOR CORRECTION CAN EVEN BE EFFECTED. THIS WAIVER OF RESPONSIBILITY INCLUDES PHOTOGRAPHIC PRINTS, POSITIVES, NEGATIVES, TRANSPARENCIES, MOVIES, AND ANY OTHER PHOTOGRAPHIC MEDIUM, MATERIAL, OR PRODUCT.

(18) ALL PROOFS, PREVIEWS, APPROVAL PHOTOGRAPHS, NEGATIVES, TRANSPARENCIES, AND MOVIES, ARE THE PROPERTY OF THE STUDIO UNLESS OTHERWISE SPECIFIED HEREIN:

____

____

THESE NOTED ITEMS, WHEN SUBMITTED TO THE PURCHASER OR REPRESENTATIVE FOR APPROVAL, MUST BE RETURNED TO THE STUDIO WITHIN:

____

ALL MATERIAL NOT RETURNED TO THE STUDIO WILL BE CHARGED FOR AT THE REGULAR PRICE LIST RATE IN EFFECT AT THAT TIME.

(19) WHERE TRANSPARENCIES AND/OR MOVIES ARE TAKEN AT THE SAME TIME AS NEGATIVE MATERIALS ARE USED, THE TRANSPARENCIES AND/OR MOVIES WILL NOT BE DELIVERED TO THE PURCHASER/REPRESENTATIVE UNTIL THE COMPLETE ORDER IS PAID IN FULL.

(20) IF TRANSPARENCIES AND/OR MOVIES ONLY ARE CONTRACTED FOR, THE ENTIRE AMOUNT SPECIFIED MUST BE PAID IN FULL AT LEAST THIRTY (30) DAYS PRIOR TO THE SCHEDULED EVENT.

(21) THE ORDER FOR PRODUCTS/SERVICES CONTRACTED HEREIN MUST BE PLACED AT THE TIME THAT PROOFS/PREVIEWS/ APPROVAL PHOTOGRAPHS, OR POSITIVES ARE RETURNED TO THE STUDIO AS SPECIFIED IN ITEM #18, AND IN NO EVENT LATER THAN

____

AFTER RECEIPT OF THESE ITEMS BY THE PURCHASER OR REPRESENTATIVE. FAILURE TO COMPLY WITH THIS REQUIREMENT ENABLES THE STUDIO TO DECLARE A BREACH OF CONTRACT, WITH ALL SUMS DUE AND PAYABLE AND SUBJECT TO COLLECTION. THE STUDIO IS THEN NO LONGER OBLIGATED TO THE CONDITIONS OF THE CONTRACT.

(22) AFTER THE PURCHASER, OR REPRESENTATIVE, PLACES THE ORDER FOR THE PRODUCT(S) AND/OR SERVICE(S) SPECIFIED UNDER THE BASIC CONTRACT, THE STUDIO, UNLESS AFFECTED BY MATERIAL SHORTAGES, SPECIAL CUSTOMER REQUESTS, LABOR SHORTAGES, OR CIRCUMSTANCES BEYOND ITS CONTROL, WILL DELIVER THESE SAME PRODUCTS/SERVICES TO THE PURCHASER/REPRESENTATIVE NO LATER THAN:

____

____

PROVIDING THAT THE PURCHASER OR REPRESENTATIVE HAS FULFILLED ALL OF HIS OBLIGATIONS AS STATED AND AGREED UPON IN THIS CONTRACT.

(23) FOR VALUABLE CONSIDERATION(S) RECEIVED, THE STUDIO IS GRANTED PERMISSION TO DISPLAY OR PUBLISH ANY PHOTOGRAPH(S) TAKEN AT THIS EVENT:

____

(24) A COPY OF THIS SHEET WILL BE IN THE POSSESSION OF THE PRINCIPAL PHOTOGRAPHER. ADDITIONAL REQUESTED SERVICES AND QUOTED COSTS WILL BE NOTED ON THE REVERSE SIDE AND SIGNED BY THE AUTHORIZING PERSON(S). FULL PAYMENT FOR SUCH ADDITIONAL SERVICES IS DUE AND PAYABLE AS SOON AS THE EVENT HAS BEEN CONCLUDED, OR SUCH SERVICE HAS BEEN RENDERED, AND PRIOR TO THE DEPARTURE OF THE PHOTOGRAPHER FROM THE PREMISES.

(25) IN THE EVENT LITIGATION BECOMES NECESSARY TO ENFORCE ANY OF THE CONDITIONS OF THIS CONTRACT, THE STUDIO SHALL BE REIMBURSED FOR ALL EXPENSES INCLUDING ATTORNEY(S) FEES AND COURT COSTS.

(26) IF LITIGATION INSTITUTED BY THE PURCHASER OR REPRESENTATIVE IS ADJUDICATED FOR THE STUDIO, THEN SAID STUDIO SHALL BE REIMBURSED FOR ALL EXPENSES INCLUDING ATTORNEY(S) FEES AND COURT COSTS.

(27) ADDITIONAL SHEETS MAY BE ADDED TO THIS CONTRACT AS REQUIRED. ALL SUCH ADDITIONS WILL BE SIGNED BY THE PURCHASER OR REPRESENTATIVE AND BY AN AUTHORIZED REPRESENTATIVE OF THE STUDIO. ADDITIONAL SHEETS WILL BE NUMBERED AND THESE NUMBERS NOTED ON THIS CONTRACT IN THE SPACE PROVIDED BELOW. ALL SUCH ADDITIONS TO THIS SHEET WILL BE INITIALED BY ALL PARTIES:

____

(28) REMARKS ____

____

____

(29) THE PURCHASER/REPRESENTATIVE HAS READ THIS ENTIRE CONTRACT AND ACKNOWLEDGES RECEIPT OF A COPY OF SAME.

THE TERMS OF THIS CONTRACT ACCEPTED THIS DATE ______________________ 19______

____

PURCHASER☐ REPRESENTATIVE☐

____

ADDRESS CITY STATE ZIP CODE TELEPHONE

____

Item 10 specifies the size of the staff to be used on the job. This is useful for commercial assignments.

Item 11 is very important. It is of particular benefit not only to a studio employing several photographers but also to an individual working photographer. Inclusion of this clause does away with any implication that a specific photographer will be the one doing the actual work. If a contract reads, "John Doe is hereby engaged to do the photography for . . . ," and if John Doe becomes ill and sends Mary Doe to do the work, the client can sue if the service or product is not satisfactory. In showing photographic samples to a prospective client it is important to mention that what is being shown is a *representative sampling.*

Some studios post a sign in the reception area informing customers about the assignment of photographers. While most persons will mentally file and forget it, the sign is there for them to see. The studio is not trying to mislead people by showing one photographer's samples and sending someone else to do the shooting. The point has been made: The samples are the collective works of all the studio's photographers.

Item 12 is the beginning of the heart of the business operation: money. Most people dislike the topic, many shun it; but the truth of the matter is that we all

Sometimes a printed notice can help ease an awkward situation.

ABOUT CAMERAS . . .

Your host has a contract with a professional studio. No cameras will be permitted and no photographs will be taken while the professional photographer is on the job. Thank you for your cooperation.

NEW HORIZONS PHOTOGRAPHY

live by it. Anyone taking photographs while the professional photographer is working is cutting into the actual dollar amount of that job. If an amateur captures the photographer's setup on his own film, then he can reproduce those professionally arranged shots at a fraction of the cost of purchasing the photograph from the studio.

Item 12 also works in conjunction with Item 16, which will be explained in its place. Some photographers distribute cards to camera-carrying guests, asking them please to refrain from taking pictures while the professional is working. The figure illustrates the "notice" distributed by New Horizons Photography. (See Chapter 19 for fuller details on this subject.)

Item 13 is where the studio or the independent photographer is protected against bad checks, faulty payments, and other financial problems with the client. The deposit should be large enough to discourage the client from price-shopping after the contract has been signed. In many states the *cancellation fee* can be retained, although *deposits* must be returned, as explained previously. Item 13 works in conjunction with Item 14, and a deposit of one third of the total contract amount is not unfair. Another third is due before the taking of the photographs. The final third is payable upon delivery of the proofs, at which time, under this payment schedule, the entire amount due under the basic contract will have been paid. With the stipulation that additional orders must be paid in full when the order is placed with no c.o.d.'s or balances due, the protection circle is complete.

Item 14 works in conjunction with Item 13. Insert the amount of the deposit as a cancellation fee. This will keep people from shopping after signing the contract. The cancellation fee reimburses the photographer for the time spent with the client in preliminary discussions, travel to the client's residence or place of business in cases where the client does not go to the photographer's studio or other place of business. Remember that some states, such as California, have consumer-protection laws specifying that the consumer has 72 hours in which to cancel a sales contract concluded away from the seller's place of business. Remember also that cancellation fees are exempt from this ruling. Although the law was enacted to protect consumers from high-pressure door-to-door salespeople, consumers have taken advantage of the law for their own purpose by doing comparison shopping at home, giving out small deposits, and then canceling all but the selected vendor.

Item 15 is a double-sided protection clause. It protects the photographer in the event of any failure to take or to deliver any photographs. It does not limit itself to equipment failure, as do many other contracts currently in use. It is a product-liability clause. At the same time it guarantees to the client that if something precludes delivery of the items specified in the contract then the client will receive a full refund of all monies paid.

Item 16 is self-explanatory. It states that if the photographer is hampered in any way in doing his job he can walk off the job without completing his assigned duties. Go back to Item 12 and see how the combination of these two paragraphs will guarantee that snapshooters will not hamper the photographer on the job. A short reminder to the contracting party to speak to the camera-carrying guest will usually end any actual interference. (See the anecdote in Chapter 19.)

Item 17 was added to the original contract because of the anomalous reflectance described in Chapter 2.

Item 18 informs the client that all working materials belong to the studio. For assignments where the client actually pays for the materials on a separate schedule, or for movies that will actually be given to, and retained by, the client, space is provided to make a notation to that effect. The courts have ruled that, in the absence of an agreement to the contrary, the paying customer owns all the materials, including the negatives. The photographer has the right to retain the negatives but cannot make any use of them without the customer's permission. The customer owns everything, including the right to copyright the photograph(s), as is clearly stated in §101 and §201 of the copyright law that became effective on January 1, 1978.

Item 19 is another protective clause for the studio or photographer. With the advent of color copiers, inexpensive color prints can be made from the original prints or transparencies while you wait. If positives (color transparencies) are shot at the same time as negative materials (for black-and-white or color prints) and the transparencies are delivered to the client ahead of the print order, there is nothing to prevent a client's making prints from the transparencies and ducking all or part of the print order.

Item 20 protects the studio in cases where the job is contracted, paid for by check, and shot on the same or the following day. A good example would be payment on Friday for a weekend shooting, or shooting on the weekend with immediate payment. The transparencies or movies are usually processed overnight. That means that the product can be delivered before the client's check has had a chance to go through the banking computer system. If it is a bad check, it may take from four days to two weeks to be returned to the depositor. By this time the client has the transparencies or movies and the studio will have to resort to legal action—if the client can be found.

If the foregoing sounds foolish to the uninitiated, the following is an actual happening.

The wedding was contracted two weeks ahead of the event. Most of the arrangements were made by telephone. The bride's father said he would mail $100 deposit checks to the band, the photographer, and the florist. He gave a $250 check to the catering establishment. By the day before the event none of the vendors had received the promised deposits, and phone calls were made to the host. He said he had been very busy with the arrangements and would issue checks for the full amount when the vendors arrived on location.

True to his word, the host did pay everyone in full. The day was Saturday. After the wedding the host thanked everyone for making the event a beautiful affair. On Monday the checks were deposited and the matter was considered closed. On this same Monday, the studio received a telephone call from the host. The newlyweds were leaving for France on Thursday and wanted to take the transparencies with them to show to relatives. As long as the contract had been paid in full, could the studio please rush the pictures? The client was not in a rush for the album of prints, which could be delivered at a later date.

Anything wrong with that? Not so far. The client stopped in at the studio on Wednesday and picked up the transparencies. He again thanked the photographer and left.

On Thursday morning the bottom fell out of the barrel. The caterer's check for more than $3000 bounced, the florist's check for $550 bounced, the band's check for $750 bounced, and the photography studio's check for $700 bounced. Telephones were busy as each one called the others. All the checks except the original $500 deposit paid to the caterer were bad.

It turned out that the checking account had been closed just before the bank closed on Friday, the day before the wedding. The family had vacated their rented house on Sunday, the day after the wedding. There was no trace of them. It had taken three full days for the checks to be returned to the depositors' banks with the notation that the account was closed. One irony was that two of the vendors banked with the same institution as the fleecer. They were at a different branch, though, and it still took three days for the checks to go through that bank's own system.

All checks must clear through the payer's bank and be credited to the payee's account prior to completion of any stipulated phase of the contract. If you have two thirds banked and the last third goes bad, at least your expenses are, or should be, covered. You would stand to lose your profit, which is bad enough; but loss of the profit is better than loss of the entire amount.

Item 21 partly eliminates the delay in customer returns of the photographic materials offered for approval before the finished products are ordered. A time limit, together with a breach-of-contract clause, will eliminate all except a minute number of "foot-draggers." The draggers can usually be rounded up with one or two telephone calls.

Item 22 is a unique clause in a business contract. It protects the customer, and only the customer. Many studios, and individual photographers, are negligent in the way they attend to customers once the photographs have been taken. There is no reason for a bride not to receive her complete order within two months after the proofs are returned with the print order. If a special album has been ordered, and that is causing the delay, that is understandable. However, to run a business on a regular delay basis is inexcusable.

Item 23 covers normal display of social-event photographs, up to a certain point. Even though the contracting party has given permission to display photographs taken at the event, any individual included in any picture can insist the studio remove that photograph from display. The best insurance is a standard *model-release* form.

For commercial assignments, Item 23 must be eliminated: The photographer cannot display or publish the photograph(s) without permission of the client and also a properly executed model release.

Item 24 covers additional requests that are made on location. The second side of the contract is photocopied and carried by the photographer. All additional requests for photographs are noted on the blank side and approved in writing by the contracting party. This sheet is attached to the original contract when the photographer returns to the studio after the event (see Items 27 and 28).

Item 25 covers collection of expenses incurred by the studio as a result of any litigation that might be needed to enforce any part of the contract.

Item 26 is a "turn-about" clause. If a client sues the studio, the studio must incur expenses in providing a defense. Advance knowledge that the loser is liable for all attorney fees and court costs will eliminate all but the most legitimate lawsuits from dissatisified clients.

Item 27 provides a convenient place to list all additional sheets that may be attached as part of the contract. For example, notes on extended travel arrangements or job specifications. (Also see Item 24).

Item 28 is a catch-all space that can be used as an adjunct for any of the listed items–Item 24 is one such. The space could be used in lieu of using a copy of the contract on the job, as described above under Item 24.

Item 29 is needed to show that the customer has read the contract and has received a copy of it. The client, or customer, also indicates acceptance of the terms stated. The contracting party should sign his or her name on the line provided for this purpose, and also type or print the name legibly.

The Bottom Line

That is the entire business contract. It is a comprehensive document which leaves nothing open to misinterpretation and which should form the basis upon which the business is operated. Other useful contractual agreements are discussed in Chapter 8.

CHAPTER 4

The Filing System

An efficiently operated business is one where orders flow easily, customers' files and materials are coordinated efficiently, and every facet of the business is keyed to a high standard of operation. The business contract is the document that sets the entire system in operation through the *contract number.*

With a centralized numbering system it is possible to throw 1000 negatives, invoices, photographic prints, and job-associated papers from ten different jobs into one pile and then sort everything into the respective clients' files in the right order.

The central numbering system based on the contract number also extends to future orders a client may place. One person called the studio six years after a particular wedding, wanting additional photographs. The name did not strike a responsive chord, but when the album number—the same as the contract number—was mentioned, the file was found within two minutes. The difference between finding a customer's file within minutes and hunting through cartons, boxes, and slipshod records can spell the difference between additional profits and "No Sale."

While the contract number forms the basis for the numbering system, additional notations are made to accommodate business conditions. Take any basic contract number—say, 2601. If this were for a wedding, the number would be used as shown. For commercial assignments, the letter "C" would be added: 2601C. Legal photography assignments would be indicated by "L"—2601L. Of course each individual photographer or studio manager can choose suffixes appropriate to the assignments.

All contracts are numbered in succession from a chosen starting point, yet the system can be varied to your own needs or desires. In this successive numbering system, with a starting base of 2601 in our example the next assignment will be 2602, followed by 2603, 2604, etc. If 2605 is a commercial job, then the file (and contract) number becomes 2605C. Let us assume that 2607 is a legal photography assignment—that file number becomes 2607L.

Setting Up the Master File

With those numbers as basics, let us now set up our system. The *Master Number List* contains all the contract numbers. A 4″ X 6″ card file is very handy. Prepare cards in groups of 100 or more numbers at a time. It is then easy to identify the next available contract number. The accompanying illustration shows a sample card. The client's name is placed on the same line as the number, which will now appear on everything related to that client. Suffix letters are added as the jobs are contracted.

Next, make up an individual card for each client. Notice in the illustrations that follow the differences among the cards for social, commercial, and legal assignments. The client's card contains the following information: Name, address, telephone number (including the person's business telephone number, if available), the contract number, and the event and date. In the case of a wedding, the bridegroom's full name is shown.

The Master Number List can be kept on file cards.

FILE NO.	NAME	MASTER NUMBER LIST
2601	SMITH, MR. & MRS. JOHN	
2602	MAXWELL, MISS ALICE	
2603	GALLOWAY, MR. ARNOLD	
2604	ELTON, MR. & MRS. DAVID	
2605C	JONES ENTERPRISES	
2606	STEWART, MS ROBIN	
2607L	JACKSON, O'CONNELL, PHILLIPS	
2608	MARTIN, WILLIAM	
2609C	STEVENS CORP.	
2610L	ROTH, JERRY	
2611C	FRANKLIN ADVERTISING AGENCY	
2612		
2613		

SMITH, MR. & MRS. JOHN (MARION)

824 Mountian View Dr.
Calabasas, CA 91302
Tel: (213)555-1212

FILE	EVENT	DATE
2601	Wedding: Cindi	6/23/79
/2	Sweet Sixteen party: Janet	9/16/79

Each client has a card, filed alphabetically

If you receive another assignment from the same client, such as another wedding, a bar mitzvah, or a party, you *do not take another contract number*: You use the same number—with *suffixes.* Thus, the second job with the Smiths would have contract number 2601/2, the third job would carry the number 2601/3, and so on.

Commercial jobs would follow the same basic pattern. The first Jones Enterprises assignment would be 2605C, the second would be 2605C/2, the third would be 2605C/3, etc. Assignments from a law firm would be shown as: 2607L, 2607L/2, 2607L/3, etc. Those are your basic contract numbers.

The cards for commercial and legal clients differ from the cards for private customers, as shown in the accompanying illustrations. There is a first card, containing the primary client's name, address, business telephone number, and the name of the person to contact. The *primary client* is your contracting client, such as an attorney. The second, and any subsequent, card has the primary client's name on the top line, in capi-

A commercial client may have an alphabetical reference . . .

```
JONES ENTERPRISES                          CARD #1
--------------------------------------------------
                                       FILE 2605C
1220 Milburn Ave.
Simi, CA 93063
Tel: (805)555-1212
Terri Anderson, Purchasing
```

. . . and also a separate card showing specific assignments.

```
JONES ENTERPRISES                          CARD #2
--------------------------------------------------
FILE NO. 2605C                             DATE
2605C     Wall Cabinets                    2/2/79
     /2   Small kitchen products           2/21/79
     /3   Hangers                          3/14/79
     /4   Lighting fixtures                5/18/79
```

JACKSON, O'CONNELL, & PHILLIPS CARD #1

FILE 2607L

Attorneys at Law
18500 Rodeo Drive
Beverly Hills, CA 90212
Tel: (213)853-1212

Frank Jackson, Kathy O'Connell, Edward Phillips

Legal clients are given an "L" suffix.

tal letters. On the extreme right side of the first card (on the top line) is the notation "Card #1", with the contract (or file, or job) number below it. On Card #2, the basic contract number is given as a column heading: 2605C. Then individual assignments, with the subject matter and dates, are shown. When Card #2 is filled, a Card #3 is begun. The form is similar for legal clients.

Now for the Record Files

The most efficient way to store your customer information is in a regular filing cabinet. Full suspension drawers are highly recommended. This type of construction makes it easier to operate heavy-laden drawers. The extra initial investment is well worth the difference. The choice between two-drawer and four-drawer cabinets will depend as much upon the space available as upon the number of clients expected. Letter-size cabinets will probably be better than legal size.

At the same time you make the client card, prepare a letter-size folder with the customer's name and

JACKSON, O'CONNELL, & PHILLIPS		CARD #2
FILE NO. 2607L		DATE
2607L	Harold Franklin	3/10/79
/2	Margaret Mason	3/15/79
/3	Lannie Baker	4/1/79
/4	Eric Mann	4/18/79
/5	Cary Stevens	4/22/79
/6	Nina Martinez	5/4/79
/7	Scott Nelson	5/19/79
/8	Kim Thompson	5/22/79

The second legal-client card lists "cases" in order by date.

the basic contract number, as in the accompanying illustration. These can be filled alphabetically, or sections can be made for social, commercial, legal, and other specialty assignments. Labels can be striped in an identifying color with a marker pen, or bought preprinted with color stripes in stationery-supply stores. With a color system for filing you can use a plain label for social assignments, yellow for commercial, blue for legal, and so forth. Sometimes an expandable "file pocket" is needed to hold all a client's material.

After several years all files should be cleaned out. Folders of nonactive clients should be transferred to inexpensive storage boxes and placed in some out-of-the-way area for storage. The notation "Storage", the date, and the number and location of the box should then be marked on the customer's file card. Then, if you ever have to find a client's file, the file card will tell you exactly where it is.

This is the basic filing system, upon which much of what follows will depend. It is also a part of the accounting system (see Chapter 9) and of the system of communications.

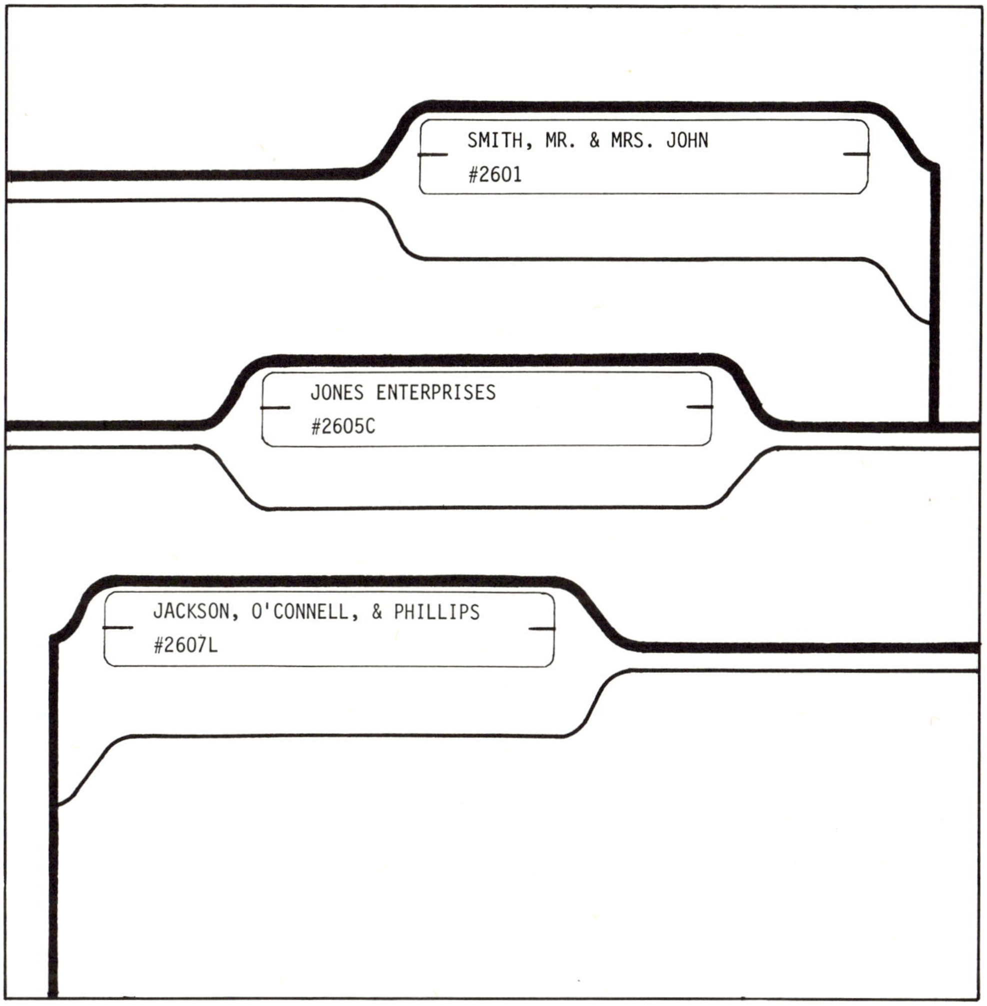

Client's name and number identify the file folders in which their records are kept.

Proof-Negative Index

CHAPTER 5

The terms *proof* and *preview* are used interchangeably by many photographers. A preview print is actually a proof, but the term *preview* seems to be more acceptable to some photographers who sell these prints for additional revenue. (More about this in Chapter 20.)

Indexing Negatives

The negative or transparency is the first material product of a photography assignment. Because of the amount of work involved in handling negatives, we shall begin with that.

If film is processed in-house, leave it in one continuous strip per roll. Whether it is a commercially packaged roll or a studio-loaded cartridge, the important thing is to have the film uncut, in a strip. If the film is processed by a commercial lab, then write "Do not cut film" on your processing order.

If feasible, try to arrange the film in the same sequence as it was shot.

The contract number becomes the base number. Again taking 2601 as the job number for this example, the first negative would be number 2601-1, the second would be 2601-2, and the series would continue 2601-3, 2601-4, 2601-5, and so on until the last negative, which might be as high as 2601-120. This is the *successive numbering* method, and you are putting your own numbers on the negatives. The same numbering system can be used with sheet films.

Another method is to utilize the numbers placed on the film during manufacture. There are advantages and drawbacks to that method, as we shall see. Each roll of 2¼″ film will have numbers along the edge. These numbers, from 1 through 12 on size 120 film and 1 through 24 on size 220 film, are spaced to correspond to the frames. Using the *consecutive numbering* system, we simply add our own number in the border (disregarding the factory number) as shown in the accompanying figure. The numbered roll-film negatives are now cut into strips of two, four, or more as desired.

All negatives should be numbered in the margins as soon as they are processed.

NEGATIVE NUMBERING

CUT FILM & ROLL FILM

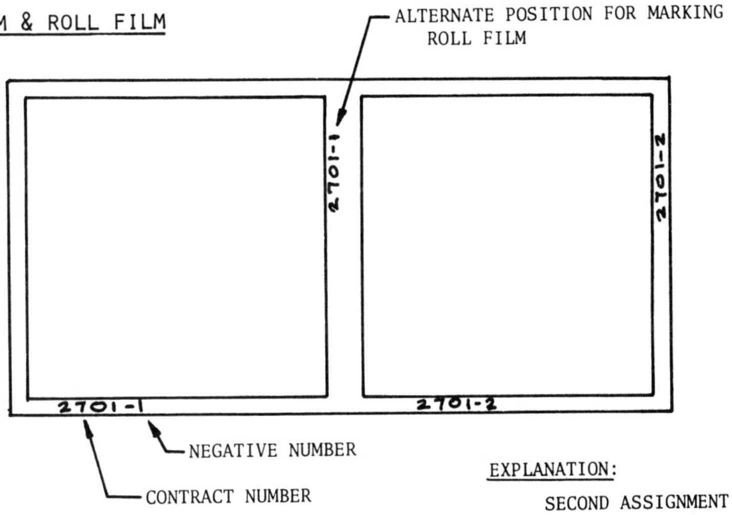

EXPLANATION:

SECOND ASSIGNMENT FOR SAME CLIENT WOULD BE NUMBERED AS FOLLOWS: 2701/2-1, 2701/2-2, ETC.

35 MM FILM IDENTIFICATION

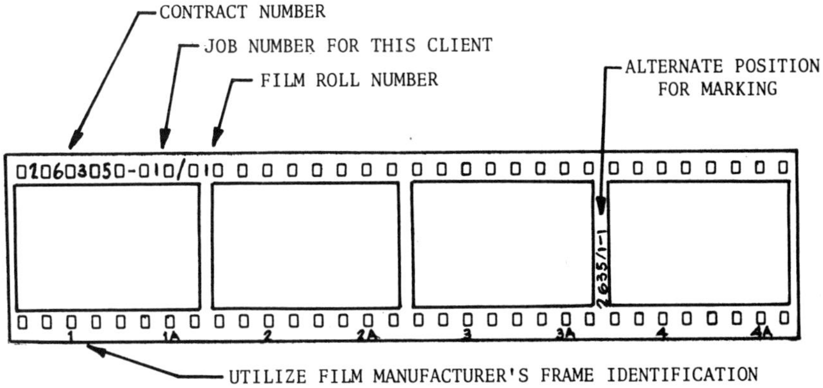

EXAMPLE: 2635-1/1-1 = CONTRACT #2635, FIRST ASSIGNEMNT, ROLL #1, FRAME #1
2635-2/1-1 = CONTRACT #2635, SECOND ASSIGNEMNT, ROLL #1, FRAME #1

A slightly different system is needed for 35 mm film. Both edges of 35 mm film are pretty well taken up by sprocket holes, leaving little or no room for adding any notations except between the holes. You will find that 35 mm negatives are factory-numbered along the bottom edge. There are two sets of numbers: 1, 2, 3, 4, etc., and 1A, 2A, 3A, 4A, etc. According to where the frames fall, you can select either set of numbers to work with. It is easier to use the factory numbers on 35 mm film, and add your own identifying numbers as you cut the film into strips of convenient size for your storage system—usually either 4 or 6 frames to a strip. As shown in the accompanying figure, the rolls are numbered: 2601/1, 2601/2, 2601/3, etc. Each strip of each individual roll of 35 mm film would carry the same number. For example, if you have a roll of 36 exposures cut into six strips of six frames each—the first roll taken on job number 2601—then you would number *all* the strips 2601/1. Similarly, *all* the strips of the second roll shot would be 2601/2, and those of roll number three would be 2601/3. Then, if you were to toss all the 35mm negatives into one pile you would be able to separate them by the contract number and roll number.

While the 35 mm *repetitive numbering* method can also be used with 120 or 220 roll film, it should only be used as a last resort, or if the rolls of film are not going to be cut into combinations of two, four, or six negatives.

Marking Prints

The next step is to match the negatives with the prints and place the negatives numbers on the backs of the corresponding prints. There are several methods for placing identifying marks on negatives and prints. The choice is entirely up to the individual photographer.

India ink and a drawing pen can be used, or marking pens made for the purpose are available at photo-supply stores or through mail-order concerns. Some of the pens contain ink that can be removed with liquid eradicator, while others are permanent. The drawing pen is available with a variety of line widths, which makes it useful for numbering negatives.

Another marking method is a hot stamp numbering machine. This is excellent for studios that have a large volume of business because the machines can be set up to stamp any system of numbers, although special marks, such as the slash line (/), may have to be custom fitted by the manufacturer of the machine.

Prints can be marked with ink pens or with rubber stamps. The regular rubber-stamp inks are not compatible with resin-coated papers, so be sure to get the special marking inks.

There is one important thing to keep in mind: What has been presented is a guide. If it works for you, then it is good. If you can use it to devise your own system, then that is what you should do. No one system can work for everyone, and there should never be any hard-and-fast rules. Try a system for a while. If you don't like it, change it. Change it once or several times, until you get a system you feel comfortable with.

How to Set Up the Index

If proof prints are delivered to the customer in loose fashion, such as in an envelope, then the numbering job has been completed, and you can skip this section. If you use albums or books to present proofs or previews to your customer, read on here.

The *Proof-Negative Index* (which is shown on the next page) is used as a cross reference. The sheet is numbered from 01 to 00 and preprinted in stock quantities. Next, the proofs are arranged in the presentation book in the numbered places. If the prints are arranged in storybook fashion rather than in the order in which the photographs were taken, then the *proof numbers* the customer sees will not correspond to your *negative numbers*. Some proof-presentation books have ordering pages interleaved with the print pages. Although some photographers write the negative numbers on those pages, and customers write their photo orders on those same pages, it is better to discourage any writing where the preview photograph becomes the base for the paper you write upon. The

Proof-Negative Index

The Proof-Negative Index serves as a cross-reference.

PROOF/PREVIEW-NEGATIVE INDEX

NAME:

CONTRACT #

SH OF

	PROOF PREVIEW	NEGATIVE NUMBER		PROOF PREVIEW	NEGATIVE NUMBER		PROOF PREVIEW	NEGATIVE NUMBER		
	01			37			73			
	02			38			74			
	03			39			75			
	04			40			76			
	05			41			77			
	06			42			78			
	07			43			79			
	08			44			80			
	09			45			81			
	10			46			82			
	11			47			83			
	12			48			84			
	13			49			85			
	14			50			86			
	15			51			87			
	16			52			88			
	17			53			89			
	18			54			90			
	19			55			91			
	20			56			92			
	21			57			93			
	22			58			94			
	23			59			95			
	24			60			96			
	25			61			97			
	26			62			98			
	27			63			99			
	28			64			00			
	29			65						
	30			66						
	31			67						
	32			68						
	33			69						
	34			70						
	35			71						
	36			72						

print can be ruined. Remember that proofs and preview albums are salable items. Numbers can be applied to the acetate pages with pressure-sensitive labels available in stationery stores.

If the job has more than 100 negatives, add a second P-N Index sheet by placing the numeral "1" in front of the preprinted numbers so that 01 becomes 101, 02 becomes 102, and so on. If three sheets are required, then make the first digit a "2"–01 becomes 201, etc. Thus, one preprinted stock item will furnish all the Proof-Negative Index sheets you need.

As each photograph is inserted into the consecutively numbered album, the *proof number* shown on the album page is marked on the P-N Index beside the corresponding *negative number*, which is the number marked on the reverse side of the print. Proof number 1 may be negative number 1, but proof number 3 may turn out to be negative number 115. If you add the proof number to the back of the print as you place it in the album (P2, P15, etc.) you have a complete circle of cross references. (For an instance where this can be crucial, see Chapter 6.)

Using the Proof Album

The easiest method of filling the customer's order after the proofs are returned is to remove the chosen photographs from the proof book and use them as your working prints. These are the prints that get marked for cropping, dodging, burning, or any special lab service. After checking the customer's list against the prints removed from the presentation book, take out the remaining prints and put them in an envelope identified with the customer's name and contract number and notation "Rejected Proofs" or some similar phrase. This now separates the "dead" prints from the working ones.

Some photographers may ask why we have removed all the prints from the presentation album. What happens in cases where we are going to sell the proof album? It is suggested that a fresh, clean album be used for this purpose. After going the rounds of family members and friends, the album is a bit worn-looking.

We now have our basic working tools: the negative and the proof print. The blank columns on the P-N Index sheet are for comments or notations. Special lab instructions may be noted. When used in conjunction with transparencies, the fact that a certain transparency was sent to a client, or accepted by the client for reproducton, can be noted. If transparency No. 3 was the one sent to the client and there are four transparencies of the same pose, then the following system can be used: Draw a bracket indicating the set, then write "To Client" after the number "3." This will show that the original went to the client, that there were four transparencies in that set, and that the remaining three are in the file. There are countless variations possible to this system. With the basic form, you can easily devise your own system.

How to File Film

What do you do with the negatives and prints in the file? Well, you could throw them into the file folder in any manner, or you could follow your new training of being systematic and use envelopes. There are special envelopes that labs use when returning cut film strips and small prints up to approximately 5″ × 5″ in size. The envelopes have two pockets and are useful for filing negatives, prints, and transparencies in the client's folder or "file pocket."

Handling Transparencies

Transparency handling is simpler than negative handling. The negative is an intermediate step in reaching a final product, the print, whereas in most instances the transparency itself is the final product, as far as the photographer is concerned. The transparency is the product that is delivered to the client.

Some photographers may question the keeping of records of transparencies on the Print-Negative Index form. The reason is that a record should be maintained of *every* photograph taken for a client, presented to a client for approval, delivered to a client, or kept behind in the file, and this is an easy way to do it.

Some photographers mount all their transparencies, regardless of whether they are 35 mm,

4″ × 5″, or 8″ × 10″. Any identification can be marked on the mounting. Eastman Kodak returns all 35 mm transparencies mounted in cardboard frames, numbered, and dated. This practice, it should be pointed out, also applies to other sizes of film: 126, 2¼″ roll film, etc. The client's contract number can be marked upon the cardboard frame, as can the name of the product, the model, or any other information—that is the choice of the individual photographer.

Transparencies are much easier to work with in filing systems.

The P-N Index is a simple system. It will help you to organize your work.

Order Forms

CHAPTER 6

An *order form* (a written purchase order) is one method of communication between the customer and the photographer or the studio. Verbal instructions can be misunderstood, mentally misplaced or forgotten, or sometimes not transmitted at all. Once committed to writing, the order is either right or wrong, with no gray areas in between. An order is written, placed, and filled. If any errors surface when the product is delivered, then they are easily traceable.

The Album Order

Let us consider noncommercial clients first—say, an album of photographs. (See the next chapter and Chapter 20 for more about albums.) Most wedding photographs, and those taken at a bar mitzvah, are usually part of a package that includes the album. For this purpose the *Albums Only* form, shown in the accompanying figure, is used.

As with every document or other piece of paper connected with a job, the job, or contract, number is entered in the appropriate space. The client's name is also shown. If more than one sheet is used for the order, this fact is shown by numbering each sheet as part of a total package of the same order form: *Sheet 1 of 3, Sheet 2 of 3, Sheet 3 of 3.* If only a single sheet is used, then it is helpful to show it as *Sheet 1 of 1.* (The abbreviation *SH* can be used in place of the full word *sheet.*) Seeing *SH 1 of 1* immediately tells you that you have the entire order on that single sheet.

The customer lists the proof numbers of the desired photographs, one number to each line. If the album will contain photographs of a single size, such as 8″ × 10″, then no other notations need be made. Each noted proof will make up the final album. If the album is to be made up of mixed sizes, then those sizes can be shown as column headings. The customer places a check mark in the appropriate column for that proof number. Albums for parents and grandparents are usually of one size photograph. If parents or grandparents desire mixed size photographs, then a separate *Album Only* order form is used for each album order, with each order form clearly marked with the name of the person the album is for.

ALBUMS ONLY

NAME:

CONTRACT #

WEDDING

SH OF

PREVIEW NUMBER	NEGATIVE NUMBER	BRIDE & GROOM			PARENTS		GRANDPARENTS			
					BRIDE	GROOM	BRIDE	BRIDE	GROOM	GROOM

ALBUMS ONLY

NAME:

CONTRACT #

BAR/BAT MITZVAH

SH OF

PREVIEW NUMBER	NEGATIVE NUMBER	BAR/BAT MITZVAH			PARENTS	GRANDPARENTS				

Unused columns can be used for other notations for the studio or photographer only. "In Lab" would mean that that particular negative was prepared and sent to the lab. "W/Proof" would indicate that a marked proof print went along with the negative. By like token, incoming lab shipments can be checked off on these same sheets. The studio then knows exactly what has gone out and what has returned. Errors are reduced to a minimum.

The bar mitzvah *Albums Only* order form is utilized in the same manner as the wedding form. Because there may be two sets of grandparents, or a combination of one or two from either or both maternal or paternal sides, there are two columns shown for grandparents.

Single-Photo Orders

All photographs for noncommercial clients other than those to be mounted in albums are ordered on the form marked *Additional Photographs.* The same basic identification system is used: contract number, customer's name, and sheet numbers. You will note, in the figure on page 50, that 16″ × 20″ has been marked in the columnar heading. This was purposely done to encourage the client to order larger photographs. If you wish, you can start with 20″ × 24″, or any other print size. Following down the scale, and to the right of 16″ × 20″, the photographer should insert the sizes commonly handled by the studio: 8″ × 10″ (or 10″ × 10″), 5″ × 7″, 5″ × 5″ (or 4″ × 5″), and the always popular "wallet" size. Of course, you will list the sizes you use in your business. Those listed here are examples only.

Lab notes can be placed in one of the unused columns. As in the other order forms, a wide latitude has been left for the needs of various businesses. If any photograph is to be framed, then that information, too, can be shown on the order form beside the photograh number.

On all the forms under discussion there is a blank column just to the right of the *Proof/Preview*, or *Approval Photograph*, column. This column is marked after the forms are returned to the studio. The negative number is inserted in that column, as shown in the accompanying figure.

ADDITIONAL PHOTOGRAPHS

NAME:

CONTRACT # SH OF

PREVIEW NUMBER	NEGATIVE NUMBER	16" x 20"						

This is where the *Proof-Negative Index* is again referred to. Opposite each customer-marked proof number insert the corresponding negative number as copied from the P-N Index. Now the order forms should show two numbers: the customer's proof number and the all-important negative number. Once the proofs have been removed from the presentation book, the proof numbers are "lost," for all practical purposes, unless they have been marked on the back of the print at the time of insertion into the presentation album. The negative number is always the studio's basic number because it contains the basic contract number, as explained in Chapter 5.

Well, then, why should anyone take the time to mark proof numbers on the backs of prints if the negative number is the all-important number? There are some instances where people remove proof prints from albums and try to arrange their own "finished" albums. One bride reported that she wanted to see how her album would look. Another gave the explanation that she could not order prints without seeing how many she would actually need. A visual arrangement was needed by these people. If the proof prints are removed from the album, juggled around, and then replaced, your Proof-Negative Index will have to be revised to match.

The General Commercial Order

Another order form is simply called *Order Form.* It is shown in the accompanying figure. This form can be used for all commercial work. Column headings can be marked with any desired notation. This is a general-purpose form that will probably be one of the most used. With the expanse of available space, cropping information, airbrush instructions, or special lab instructions can be shown for each photograph.

It is advisable to have the client sign or initial each order form. Although it really does not mean much in the way of correcting one or two incorrectly printed photographs, it could save the day in the case of a mixup in the construction of a large wedding album. It pays to know who is reponsible for an error. Where extensive special work has been done on a photograph, the costs involved may cut into the profit margin if the studio has to absorb the loss. Written work orders avoid error.

ORDER FORM

NAME:

CONTRACT # SH OF

APPROVAL PHOTOGRAPH	NEGATIVE NUMBER							

CHAPTER 7

Album Tabulation Form

The *Album Tabulation Form* contains the complete story of the album with photographs. Fast and efficient reorders are possible with this form.

Let us consider several examples of album make-ups using the *Album Tabulation Form*, or A.T.F. As on all the other forms connected with the job, the contract number is entered in the space provided for it. The client's name is printed, last name first, and the type of event is also shown: wedding, bar mitzvah, Christmas party, engagement party, social function, etc. Under the heading *Type of Photos*, the size of photographs is noted—8″ × 10″, 5″ × 7″, 5″ × 5″—or you can enter all three sizes on the same line. A single size would indicate that the album contained only that one size, while an entry 8″ × 10″, 5″ × 5″ would indicate that the album contained two sizes and so was a *mixed album.*

The first sheet of the form contains 24 numbered spaces. The second sheet contains 24 *un*numbered spaces. (See the accompanying figures.) If there are more than 24 pages in an album, then you continue on the secondary sheets, numbering each space until you have one numbered space corresponding to each album page.

If the album contains only 8″ × 10″ prints, with one photograph per page, then the negative number of the photograph is entered in the box representing that album page. In an album made up in "storybook" or sequence form, the pictures may not fall into the same numerical sequence as the order in which they were taken. For example, let us assume that the album was constructed with the specified single size of photograph. The A.T.F. would show the corresponding negative numbers: 18-2-5-24-72-115-7-9, etc. In a wedding album, of course, the processional shots will usually fall in numerical sequence. There may be a number missing because two shots were taken and the best one was used: 32-33-34-35-37-38. As you will note, number 36 is missing. One glance at the *Album Tabulation Form* will tell you where the aisle shots appear: 17-11-20-12-26-32-33-34-35-37-38-39-41-42-43-44-45-46-47-59-63-101-70. It can be seen that the aisle, or processional, shots are in the series

ALBUM TABULATION FORM

SH OF

NAME:____________________

CONTRACT NO.:____________________

EVENT:____________ DATE:________

ALBUM COMPLETED:____________________

ALBUM JACKET:________ YES ________ NO

SIZE OF PHOTOS:____________________

____

ALBUM:____________________

IMPRINT:____________________

____

*** NOTE: X IN BOX INDICATES LAST PAGE; NP INDICATES "BLANK PAGE-NO PHOTO"

1	2	3	4	5	6
7	8	9	10	11	12
13	14	15	16	17	18
19	20	21	22	23	24
25	26	27	28	29	30
31	32	33	34	35	36

ALBUM TABULATION FORM

SH OF

NAME: ______________________

CONTRACT NO.: ______________________

EVENT: ______________ DATE: ________

*** X IN BOX INDICATES LAST PAGE; NP INDICATES "BLANK PAGE-NO PHOTO"

32–47. Numbers 36 and 40 are missing, and were probably duplicates. Table shots usually follow the same pattern.

If we have a 5″ × 7″ print size, then they are usually mounted two-per-page in the large "reversible" albums. Page number 3 has two vertical photos mounted side by side. The corresponding A.T.F. box will show the negative numbers side by side. They can be separated by a slash (/) line. If the prints are horizontal, with one above the other, then the negative numbers are shown that way.

Let us consider an album that contains four 5″ × 5″ photographs per page. Starting in the upper left corner, we mark that print number in the corresponding space on the A.T.F. form, followed by the upper right, lower left, and then the lower right. From looking at the A.T.F. boxes we can tell how the prints are mounted in the album! What a helpful tool.

To summarize: In the case of a mixed album, the 8″ × 10″ prints will be represented by a single number, the 5″ × 7″ ones will be shown by two numbers, and the 5″ × 5″ or 4″ × 5″ size will have four numbers listed in each corresponding page diagram. Some albums contain six 3½″ × 5″ prints per page. In that case, the corresponding A.T.F. space will show six negative (or print) numbers.

After everything has been put together in the album, small pressure-sensitive numbered tabs are placed in an unobtrusive place on each page. Somewhere close to the binding or the inside edge is most desirable. Some album manufacturers supply a set of numbers with each album. Or they are available in stationery and art supply stores.

Other information that can be shown on the *Album Tabulation Form* is any imprint wanted and the fact that special types of masks were used on particular photographs. And don't forget to indicate the type of album, color, and any other pertinent data.

Reordering From Albums

Now you have a link between the album in the customer's possession and your studio. Let us assume Mrs. Smith telephones for an additional Photograph several months after you have delivered the album. Will you have to ask her to remove the photograph from the album and find the number on the reverse side? If the album is a sealed type, this may be impractical or impossible without damaging the album. With the system described here, however, additional ordering is a simple matter: All the customer needs is the ordering explanation sheet shown in the accompanying figure. This sheet is included with every album that leaves the studio. In fact, with this system it is possible for the album to be in one city, the explanation sheet in a second city, and the studio in a third. As

Sample layouts can be planned on the Album Tabulation Form.

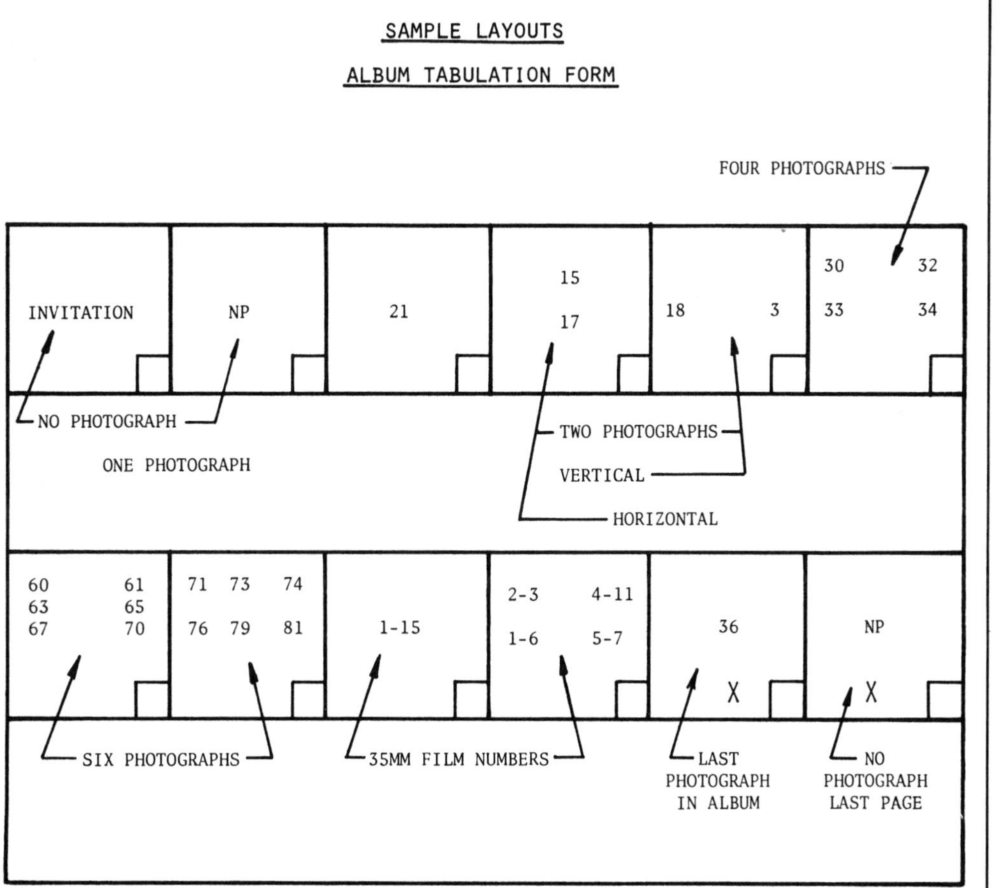

CODE:
NP = NO PHOTOGRAPH
X: WITH NUMBER = LAST PHOTOGRAPH IN ALBUM
WITHOUT NUMBER = LAST PAGE IN ALBUM; WITHOUT PHOTOGRAPH

Each client receives an instruction sheet along with the proof album.

PHOTOGRAPH ORDERING INSTRUCTIONS

When ordering additional photographs from this album, first find the album identification number as shown in the illustration.

Obtain the page number. If the numbers are missing, count the first album page as number 1. Disregard guests lists and cover sheets. Start with the first side of the first album page, which may or may not contain inserted material.

Select one of the page examples shown and match the album page where the desired photograph(s) appear(s).

In ordering, give the album number, page number, and the corresponding photograph identification letter.

For example: 2601, page 6, photograph B

One photograph on the page: 2601, page 2

If more than one photograph is ordered from the album at the same time, the album identification number is given only once.

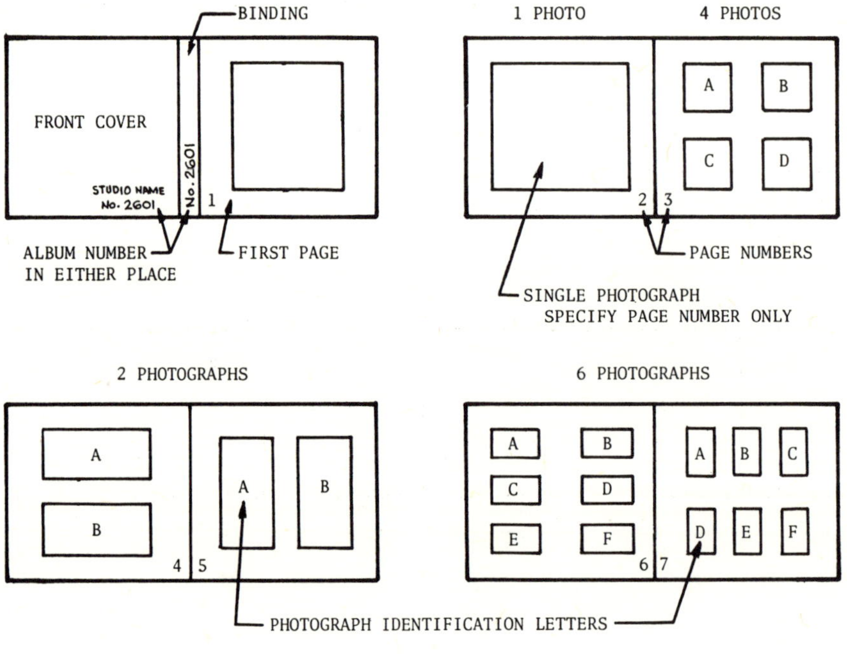

NEW HORIZONS PHOTOGRAPHY · 10409 VALLEY DRIVE · GRANADA HILLS, CA 91344 · TEL:(213)555-1212

long as everyone understands how to use the simple system, anyone can do the ordering.

Let's take another example. The customer wants the upper right photo on page 2, the lower left on page 15, and the single photo on page 25. However, the requested print sizes are different from those in the album. The upper right one on page 2 and the lower left one on page 15 are 5″ × 5″ prints. The customer wants an 8″ × 10″ of the one on page 2 and a 5″ × 7″ of the one on page 15. Wallet-size photos are desired of the photograph on page 25. All the customer has to tell the photographer, or the studio order taker, is, "I want an 8 × 10 of number 2B, a 5 × 7 of number 15C, and three wallets of number 25." We are assuming that the customer has already identified the job by the contract number and the client's name. Actually, the contract number is the only identification needed. The addition of the client's name gives the studio a double check. People sometimes transpose numbers, and there may be two or more albums with the same type of photo arrangement. Therefore, the second identification is a safety factor.

One additional word about the ever-important contract number: It must be marked somewhere on the album. A good place would be directly under the studio imprint, or on the binder margin that covers the posts on post-type albums. The best place is under the studio logo, where the customer can find it easily.

If the *Customer Instruction* sheet has been lost or misplaced, you can work with the person verbally. Tell the customer to look for the page numbers, wherever you place them on albums leaving your studio. If the numbers are not on the pages for any reason, then tell the person to count the pages as with a newspaper or book. Then, verbally repeating the instructions for ordering, you work with the person until the desired print is arrived at. You have the key to service and sales with the *Album Tabulation Form.* It is a well-developed system for identification and communication.

Permissions, Disclaimers, Information Forms

CHAPTER 8

There are many variations of release agreements, or permission forms, the most notable being the *model release.* There are many different forms and many arguments for and against each one.

If you ask an attorney to draw up a contract for you he may open a book containing various forms and choose one suitable for your purpose, or he may combine features of several forms. This is what has happened to the commonly used model-release agreement. There are many identical or similar clauses in all, or nearly all, the model releases in general use in photography today.

The information in a copyrighted work, such as a book or a magazine, can not be reproduced without the permission of the copyright owner. This also applies to documents that are copyrighted individually aside from the copyrighted works in which they appear. However, no one can prevent another person from using forms that are not covered by copyright. Usually, if you take one model release and combine it with several others you are not infringing upon anyone's copyright. You are not infringing upon anyone if you use, unaltered, an entire release that is not protected by copyright. The field is really wide open with material that is not covered by copyright.

Basically, a release is supposed to give its holder certain rights. In the case of a photographer, the release is supposed to permit the photographer to be able to sell, display, publish, republish, and otherwise use photograph(s) without restrictions. In days gone by a simple statement would have sufficed. Today it is almost necessary to include a volume of legal jargon about terms and conditions in order to express the same agreement.

Why the change? Because people are more conscious of their rights, including their right to sue. Model releases are based, in law, on the right of privacy, and also on the rights of private property. If a photograph is taken for editorial purposes, and in a public place, there should be few problems. Otherwise, it is a good idea to ask any persons who can be recognized in the picture for permission to use their likeness for your own purposes.

Releasing One's Right to Privacy

The most convenient way to keep track of permissions for the use of the likeness of any person or property for reproduction, public display, publication, advertising, or any other conceivable legitimate business purpose, is to have a written, printed, or typewritten release form that can be signed by the person or persons in the photograph. In the case of a minor, the signature of a parent or guardian is required. For private property, the owner's signature is needed.

A good case in point recently involved a nationally distributed professional photography magazine, which published the photograph of a very pretty young woman on its cover. After the issue was released, the magazine was told that no release agreement had been executed. To make matters worse, the model was under the legal age of 18 at the time the photographer took the shot. The model was posing for an advertisement in the studio of a photographer authorized to take the photographs. A second photographer, who was visiting the studio, asked if he could take a few photographs. Verbal permission was given by the model, but nothing was said about commercial use of those photographs.

Suddenly everyone concerned wanted to know where the release was, why no one had checked for permissions or releases prior to acceptance for publication, and how to get out of the situation at the least possible expense. The author was the West Coast editor of the magazine at that time and arranged to have the model sign a release in exchange for several copies of the cover on which her photograph appeared. Needless to say, if the model, now of legal age, had persisted, or had instituted a lawsuit, the photographer and the publishers could have found themselves on the short end of a justifiable monetary settlement. The model had never given the photographer permission to use her photograph for profit. The magazine's employees were negligent in not ascertaining the existence of a properly executed model release.

Release forms. There are all kinds of model releases. They can be simple handwritten statements or complex printed forms. Generally speaking, a working model will sign a release, pose for the photographs, receive payment for the services rendered, and go on to the next assignment. Professional models are not looking for loopholes or legal entanglements. Again, there are exceptions. There is a case on record where a professional model sued the photographer, the advertising agency, and the manufacturer of a product for "lewd or suggestive" advertising that was offensive to her. The release signed by the model did not stipulate that she released her right to inspect any written matter that would accompany the photographs. And that is exactly what the model objected to—the words that accompanied her photograph in an advertisement of a product she posed with. It does not matter whether or not the model won her lawsuit. What does matter is the fact that a paid professional model had legal grounds of sufficient magnitude upon which to build a lawsuit.

The question that should come to every photographer's mind is: Can I afford the costs of a lawsuit? You will notice the absence of "Can I afford the legal fees even if I win the case?" The original question is all-encompassing. With that in our memory banks, we, as photographers, should always be preapred to request a model release from everyone whose photograph(s) may have some commercial value to us. Although a simple one- or two-line handwritten release is better than none, the comprehensive release is a more desirable document.

The Model Release Agreement

Now let us consider the model release itself. There are two basic types: the long form and the short form.

The short form is available in a multitude of sizes, with a multitude of word arrangements. Some are printed on 5½″ × 8½″ paper, in loose sheets or bound in pads; others are on 3″ × 5″ cards; and there are those on 8½″ × 11″ paper, among countless others.

Model-Release forms like this one are packaged commercially.

Model Release Agreement

Date____________________________

To: ____PHOTOGRAPHER

____Address

____

For valuable consideration, I hereby irrevocably consent to and authorize the use and reproduction by you, or anyone authorized by you, of any and all photographs which you have this day taken of me, negative or positive, proofs of which are hereto attached, for any purpose whatsoever, without further compensation to me. All negatives and positives, together with the prints shall constitute your property, solely and completely.

I am over 21 years of age. __________Yes or no

____
Model Signature

Address:____

____

Witnessed by:____
Signature of Witness

(If the person signing is under age, there should be a consent by parent or guardian, as follows)

I hereby certify that I am the parent or guardian of________________

____, the model named above, and for value received I do give my consent without reservations to the foregoing on behalf of him or her or them.

Dated:________________ ______________________________________
Signature of Parent or Guardian

Witnessed by:____
Signature of Witness

One version of the long form is shown in the accompanying figure of the *Model Release Agreement.* It was drawn up by the author from several forms, available in photo shops, which do not carry any copyright symbol or notation. To all of that, the author has added some phrases of his own.

Every photographer probably has his or her own preferred release form. The short form and a long, or comprehensive, form are shown in the accompanying figures. Another type includes statements applicable to photographs showing distortion, photographs that may hold the model up to ridicule, and photographs that may inspire unpleasant comments about the model. As in all documents, the user must decide how comprehensive to be. A model-release form filled with mention of derogatory terms will not encourage the

Release agreements are also available printed on small cards.

MODEL RELEASE

Date________________

For valuable consideration, I hereby irrevocably consent to and authorize the use and reproduction by you, or anyone authorized by you, of any and all photographs which you have this day taken of me, negative or positive, proofs of which are hereto attached, for any purpose whatsoever, without further compensation to me. All negatives and positives, together with the prints shall constitute your property, solely and completely.

Model____
Signature of Model

Address____________________________Phone________________

City____________________State________Zip____________

Signature of Parent or Guardian if Minor________________________

Witnessed by____
Signature of Witness

The author worked out his own form *(see page 64)**.*

MODEL RELEASE AGREEMENT

I, the undersigned, hereby give
hereinafter referred to as said Studio, their legal representatives, assigns, and those acting on their behalf and with their permission, the right and permission to copyright in any part of the world, to use, reuse, publish and republish, in conjunction with my own or a ficticious name, any photographs taken of me by said Studio or those acting on their behalf or with their permission, and any reproductions thereof, in any form, shape, or composite, in which I may be distorted in character or form, whether intentional or otherwise, and may be used in conjunction with any printed matter or advertising copy, for any purposes of trade, advertising, exhibit, publicity, or promotion, without restrictions or limitations.

I hereby release, discharge, and agree to save harmless said Studio, their assigns, legal representatives, agents, and those acting on their behalf and with their permission, from and against any liability resulting from any distortion, blurring, alteration, optical illusion, or use in composite form, whether such was intentional or otherwise, which may occur, result, or be produced in the taking of said photographs, or by processing or reproduction of the finished product, its publication or the distribution of same.

I waive the right to approve or inspect the photographs, advertising copy, or printed matter used in conjunction therewith.

I hereby warrant that I have read this release agreement in its entirety before affixing my signature thereto, and I fully understand the contents therein. I further warrant that I am of legal age and competent to contract in my own name as far as the above is concerned.

DATE: ____________________

SIGNATURE (NAME) PRINT NAME

ADDRESS CITY STATE ZIP CODE TELEPHONE

I warrant that I am the parent and/or guardian of : ______________________________,
PRINT NAME
the person named in the foregoing Release Agreement, and that I am duly authorized to act in his/her behalf. I have read the foregoing agreement in its entirety and I understand its contents. I hereby consent that the photographs taken under this agreement may be used for the purposes set forth therein.

SIGNATURE (NAME) PRINT NAME TELEPHONE

ADDRESS CITY STATE ZIP CODE

WITNESS:

model to sign. Instead, all sorts of unpleasant thoughts are likely to flash through the model's mind.

Some model releases carry the notation about "In consideration of ——." This means that the person agrees to pose, or has posed, and that some form of gratuity has been given in exchange. Many releases do not now contain that clause. If you decide to include it, then some of the "considerations" can be: one 11″ × 14″ print, the sum of $1, or any such valid recompense.

The long form mentions the use of a fictitious name by the model, and the waiver of the model's right to inspect or approve the finished photographs and any advertising copy or other printed matter that might be used with the photographs. It is important to be protected with this "wording" clause if the photograph is to be used as a display in the studio or as part of a studio advertising flyer.

Some studios have their logo imprinted on all their forms. Others use rubber stamps of their names or logos.

The best guide to keep in mind is the fact that what happens at the moment a photograph is taken may not carry over to the time when it is used. It is much easier to obtain permissions at the moment the photograph is taken.

One photographer who wanted to use a photograph couldn't find the person who posed. He lost a sale because he did not have a model release. If he had taken a few seconds to secure the release at the time he took the photograph, he would have been in command of the situation.

A properly executed model release agreement is therefore like another inexpensive type of insurance.

Legal Photography Release Agreement

The *Release Agreement* used in legal photography is similar to that used with a model. In legal photography the attorney retains full rights and possession of all prints, transparencies, and negatives. While most lawyers will leave the negatives in the possession of the studio or the photographer, it would be unwise to show any such photographs as samples of your work

The author created this form for use in his work for lawyers.

LEGAL PHOTOGRAPHY RELEASE AGREEMENT

TO:

By the direction of, and for the use of/by my attorney(s):

____

NAME(S)

____

ADDRESS SUITE CITY STATE ZIP CODE TELEPHONE

I hereby irrevocably consent to, and authorize the use and reproduction by you, by said attorney(s), by anyone authorized by either of you, or by authorized representatives of either, of any and all photographs which you have this day taken of me, negative or positive, for any purpose whatsoever, without compensation to me. I waive the right to inspect the photographs, negative or positive. All positives and negatives shall constitute the property of my attorney.

I warrant that I have read this release agreement and understand it completely.

I am ____________________ years of age.

DATE: ____________________

______________________ ______________________

SIGNATURE (NAME) PRINT NAME

____

ADDRESS CITY STATE ZIP CODE TELEPHONE

I hereby certify that I am the parent and/or guardian of the above named person, and that I have read the foregoing release agreement and agree to the terms and conditions specified therein.

______________________ ______________________

SIGNATURE (NAME) PRINT NAME

____

ADDRESS CITY STATE ZIP CODE TELEPHONE

WITNESS:

without the written permission of both the attorney and the client. Some accident victims the author has photographed were so badly injured that permission to reprint for display purposes would probably not be given.

If the person being photographed is a minor, written consent of a parent or guardian must be obtained. That affidavit is included as part of the release.

As you will note in the accompanying figure, the release states: "By the direction of, and for the use of/by, my attorney (followed by space to insert the lawyer's name, address, and telephone number), I hereby irrevocably consent to, and authorize the use and reproduction by you, by said attorney, or by anyone authorized by either of you, or by authorized representatives of either, of any and all photographs which you have this day taken of me, negative or positive, for any purpose whatsoever, without compensation to me. I waive the right to inspect the photographs, negative or positive. All negatives and positives shall constitute the property of my attorney."

Many photographers will claim ownership of the negatives. But, it has been ruled in the courts that a client who hires a photographer owns the images while the photographer retains rights of possession of the negatives. The client also retains the right of reproduction in any "work done for hire." In dealing with an attorney as the principal client, I would be prudent in handling everything concerned with use of the photographs involved.

Signatures. Many years ago the initials "L.S." were used to indicate a person's legal signature. That practice has lapsed. It is suggested that anyone signing a legal document be asked to print the name clearly as well as writing the signature. Many signatures are not much more than a scribble. It should be clear whose signature appears on the document.

The affidavit at the bottom of the release can be used for two purposes. If the person photographed is a minor, then the parent or guardian can sign. if the "extra person" is a witness instead of a guardian, simply cross out the statement pertaining to the guardian and have the witness initial the change to the document in addition to signing it.

There should be a witness to the shooting if the person photographed is of opposite gender to the photographer. Witnesses are definitely desired when the person being photographed must undress. An example is in such medical malpractice cases as breast implants. This is also applicable for accident cases where the person's body may be lacerated in places normally covered by clothing. Even if the photographer and the subject are of the same sex, it is always a good idea to have a witness present.

Inventory Photography Release Agreement

To the best of the author's knowledge, the *Premises and Contents Release Agreement* shown here stands alone in the field of release forms. It was conceived by the author in response to a need by photographers engaged in inventory-control or protection photography, where the contents of homes or businesses are photographed for purposes of record. Such purposes may be for loss due to fire, burglary, flood, or earthquake, or for the purpose of obtaining insurance coverage on valuable items.

Why should a photographer need a release in a simple matter of "doing his job?"

Well, what if the client should claim that items were missing after the photographer left, or state that an item was broken or damaged through negligence on the part of the photographer? What recourse does the studio or the photographer have if the client is burglarized, and then alleges that the studio or photographer supplied photographs of valuable items, or of the premises, to persons unknown?

The *Premises and Contents Release Agreement* clearly states that the premises and contents are in the same condition after being photographed as they were beforehand. It also states that nothing except the photographer's equipment has been removed from the premises, and that a personal examination of that equipment has been made by the party responsible. The third important statement says that all of the exposed film has been given to the person represented as the responsible party.

This agreement is comparatively short and simple, but it is very effective. One copy of the signed

Different specialties call for different forms of agreement, such as this one (by the author).

INVENTORY PHOTOGRAPHY

PREMISES & CONTENTS RELEASE AGREEMENT

I certify that I am the responsible owner/occupant/leasee/manager, or the person authorized to act in behalf of said party, of the real and/or personal property as follows: ____

____

____

____

at the following address(es):

____

STREET APT/SUITE CITY STATE ZIP CODE

____

STREET APT/SUITE CITY STATE ZIP CODE

I warrant that I was personally present at all times with the photographer(s):

____

____

while the described property was being photographed and while said photographer(s) was/were on the premises.

I further warrant that I have been given all of the film exposed on this assignment, and that said photographer(s) did not remove anything from these premises except that which they brought onto it, to wit: camera equipment, accessory photographic equipment, and unexposed film in sealed boxes or packages, and that I have personally examined all such items prior to removal from said premises.

I further warrant that the premises and/or contents are in the same condition after the photography as they were prior to said photography, and absolve the studio and its personnel, agents, and assigns, from any and all claims pertaining to loss or damage to said property, real and/or personal.

DATE: ________________

________________________ ________________________

SIGNATURE (NAME) PRINT NAME

____

ADDRESS CITY STATE ZIP CODE TELEPHONE

WITNESS: ____

NAME ADDRESS CITY STATE ZIP CODE TELEPHONE

agreement should be given to the person signing as the responsible party.

You may ask why the unprocessed film is given to the client and not processed by the studio or by the individual photographer. This is another safety feature for the studio or the photographer, as the author has explained in magazine articles on this subject.

Product and Premises Photography Release Agreement

If your client is an interior decorator, designer, product manufacturer, etc., who engages you to photograph specific items in a private residence or place of business, then another type of release agreement should be used.

The *Product and Premises Photography Release Agreement* shown in the accompanying figure states that the client gives the photographer permission to photograph the product or the premises, to enter the premises with or without escort, and to publish or use the resulting photographs without restrictions.

Although the release also transmits all rights in the photographs to the photographer, that clause may be eliminated by any of the parties. Keep in mind that any alterations to the printed form should be initialed by all parties concerned.

The *Assignment* (see illustration) should be printed on the reverse side of the release agreement.

It is important to stress the point that this release should be given to the contracting client to be completed before any photographic work is done on the premises. Above all else, the release is a permit for the photographer to enter the premises.

Photo Restorations Agreement

Photo restoration is big business. One of the current fads is the display of family photographs. Old trunks are being opened in hopes of finding photographs of relatives long since departed. Attics and basements are searched for boxes and albums of photographs taken a few years ago—or decades past.

The author designed this form so that both client and photographer

PRODUCT & PREMISES PHOTOGRAPHY
RELEASE AGREEMENT

I warrant that I am the owner/occupant/leasee/manager, or authorized representative of said party, of the property located at:

____

STREET APT/SUITE CITY STATE ZIP CODE

do hereby give permission to: ______________________________

PRINT NAME

____

ADDRESS CITY STATE ZIP CODE TELEPHONE

hereinafter known as Party B, to enter these same premises, with or without escort, to photograph the interior/exterior of said premises including external surrounding areas, and/or ______________________________

____

Party B may publish and/or display the photographs, negative or positive, color or black and white, made through any medium, without any compensation to me or to any other person(s) or companies that may in any way be associated with these premises or products. Party B is not restricted in the manner in which these photographs are to be used or for whatever purpose.

I further warrant that Party B may assign these rights and privilledges, in whole or in part, and I agree that all rights stated herein apply to said asignee(s) with the same force as they apply to Party B.

I save blameless Party B. the assigns and employees, and all others involved, from all harm and responsibility concerned with the taking, display, and/or publication of said photographs, and waive the right to inspect the photographs, negative or positive, the advertising matter, or anything used in conjunction therewith, prior to publication, display, printing, or at any time thereafter.

DATE: ____________________

______________________ ______________________

SIGNATURE (NAME) PRINT NAME

____

ADDRESS CITY STATE ZIP CODE TELEPHONE

WITNESS:

can know the exact responsibilities and limitations they agree to.

PRODUCT & PREMISES PHOTOGRAPHY
RELEASE AGREEMENT ASSIGNMENT

The agreement shown on the opposite side of this Release is assigned to:

NAME

ADDRESS CITY STATE ZIP CODE TELEPHONE

with the following restrictions:

DATE:

SIGNATURE (NAME)

PRINT NAME

ADDRESS CITY STATE ZIP CODE TELEPHONE

It is important for the person doing the work to realize, and to inform the customer, that absolutely no work is done on originals. Some persons may think that the original photograph has been restored, rather than that they are receiving a restored *copy* of the original. Most old photographs are brittle and will break under the slightest touch or pressure. The customer must understand that you assume no responsibility or

It is important that clients know what "restoration" means.

PHOTO RESTORATION AGREEMENT

It is mutually understood that in accepting the original material, whether photographic print, positive, or negative, for restorative proceedures,

hereafter known as the Studio, its employees, subcontractors, assigns, and all those acting on its behalf that will handle the original work or the restoration, that no responsibility for the physical condition of the originals is assumed, and that there is no liability implied, intended, or will be accepted in case of damage to any of the work by handling or shipping, or loss by fire, theft, or any other reason, whether or not such damage or loss was caused by negligence or any other reason whatsoever.

There is no guarantee that the restored print or work will match the original work in color, tonal gradations, or in overall size or appearance. Care will be taken to make the reproduction as close to the original as possible within limitations and restrictions as may be exercised by the restoration artist.

No restorative work is done on the original work, which will be returned to the customer together with the newly created restoration photograph or artwork.

If the restoration work does not meet with the customer's approval, one retouching will be made on the first submission only. If the customer still refused to accept the restoration print or work, then a refund of up to fifty percent (50%) of the original contracted price will be made. All materials will be retained by the Studio with the exception of the customer's original photograph or artwork, which will be returned to the customer.

The customer acknowledges that he/she has read the foregoing in its entirety, and that he/she agrees to the terms and conditions as set forth herein.

DATE:____________________

____________________________ ____________________________

CUSTOMER SIGNATURE PRINT NAME

____

ADDRESS CITY STATE ZIP CODE TELEPHONE

liability for the condition of the original, nor can you guarantee the final work in certain respects. You cannot guarantee sharpness. You cannot guarantee that tonal values of the reproduction will match the original. Reproducing sharp copies of some old photographs may not be possible.

Although many labs and restoration artists have their own forms, which may contain disclaimer notices, the *Photo Restoration Agreement* illustrated here is more protective for you, the agent in the transaction.

Information Forms

There are other forms that are either necessary or useful to a well-run business operation. The *Wedding Information* form is shown in the accompanying figure. The information can be helpful to the couple's parents in filling otu newspaper releases and also can assist the photographer on the job.

Weddings

While it may be assumed that the prospective bride and bridegroom both have parents, it cannot be assumed that the parents are paying for the wedding. It cannot be assumed that either one lives with their parents. This is a fact-gathering sheet for information purposes only. The after-the-wedding residence address of the couple can be noted in the space provided. If any of the telephone numbers is unlisted, be sure to note that fact, preferably after the number itself: (213) 555-1212 (Unl). The notation (Unl) immediately says, "This is an unlisted number—it is *not for distribution.*" Unlisted telephone numbers should never be given out to any third party. If you are ever asked for a client's telephone number, always check with the client to make sure there is no objection to giving it out.

Bar/Bat Mitzvah

This information form is used for both the bar mitzvah information for boys, and the bat mitzvah information for girls. Its purpose is the same as that of any other information form: to bring together information that will be useful to the studio and to the photographer.

WEDDING INFORMATION

BRIDE: ______________________________
PRINT FULL NAME

____
ADDRESS CITY STATE ZIP CODE TELEPHONE

PARENTS: ______________ ______________
MOTHER FATHER

______________ ______________
ADDRESS(ES)

______________ ______________
TELEPHONE NUMBERS & MISC. INFO.

GROOM: ______________________________
PRINT FULL NAME

____
ADDRESS CITY STATE ZIP CODE TELEPHONE

PARENTS: ______________ ______________
MOTHER FATHER

______________ ______________
ADDRESS(ES)

______________ ______________
TELEPHONE NUMBERS & MISC. INFO.

WEDDING: ______________ 19 ______ AM ______ PM
DAY OF WEEK MONTH DATE TIME

PLACE: ______________________________

____
ADDRESS CITY STATE ZIP CODE TELEPHONE

____
COORDINATOR OR PERSON IN CHARGE

MINISTER: ______________________________

____
ADDRESS CITY STATE ZIP CODE TELEPHONE

RECEPTION: ______________________________

____
ADDRESS CITY STATE ZIP CODE TELEPHONE

DATE: ______________ 19 ______ AM ______ PM
DAY OF WEEK MONTH DATE TIME

____
COORDINATOR OR PERSON IN CHARGE

BRIDE & GROOM AFTER WEDDING ADDRESS:

____
ADDRESS CITY STATE ZIP CODE TELEPHONE

ADDITIONAL
INFORMATION:

____

____

____

BAR/BAT MITZVAH INFORMATION

BAR/BAT MITZVAH: ____
PRINT FULL NAME

PARENTS: ____
FATHER MOTHER

____
ADDRESS CITY STATE ZIP CODE TELEPHONE

EVENT DATE: ________ 19 ________ AM PM
DAY OF WEEK MONTH DATE TIME

PLACE: ____

____
ADDRESS CITY STATE ZIP CODE TELEPHONE

____
COORDINATOR OR PERSON IN CHARGE

RABBI: ____

____
ADDRESS CITY STATE ZIP CODE TELEPHONE

RECEPTION: ____

____
ADDRESS CITY STATE ZIP CODE TELEPHONE

DATE: ________ 19 ________ AM PM
DAY OF WEEK MONTH DATE TIME

____
COORDINATOR OR PERSON IN CHARGE

BROTHERS: ____

SISTERS : ____

GRANDPARENTS: ____
MATERNAL

____
PATERNAL

ADDITIONAL INFORMATION: ____

____

____

____

____

Certain pecularities of any of the parties can be noted in the space allotted to *additional information.* For example, at one bar mitzvah the photographer addressed one of the grandparents as "Grandfather" while he was arranging various groups to be photographed. The person became angry and responded: "I am not your grandfather. How dare you address me as such? Furthermore, I do not like being called 'grandfather' by anyone, including my grandchildren. They call me by my first name." Nothing the photographer said could pacify the man. Finally he told the man he could be left out of the photographs if he so desired, or he could say what name he preferred to be called by and proceed with the photography. The man calmed down and said he preferred the use of his first name. Now, if that information had been on the information form the difficulty could have been avoided. The man's daughter later told the photographer that her father worked as an extra in the movies and did not want anyone to know his age; he felt that being a grandfather could be injurious to his career.

The Clergy Can Help

One useful bit of information on both forms is the name(s) of the clergy. You also have a telephone number where minister, priest, or rabbi can be reached. If you are unfamiliar with the ceremony you can telephone the clergy in advance and discuss the event. You can learn about any restrictions, local customs, and personal likes and dislikes. All in all, these forms can make your work a lot easier.

CHAPTER 9

Accounting and Bookkeeping

If you discuss accounting with a bookkeeper you will most likely be told that you do not need an accountant. If you discuss the same topic with an accountant you will probably be informed that bookkeepers keep books, that's all. You may be told that the accountant knows what business deductions can and cannot be taken, your depreciation schedule, and that it is the accountant who should do your tax returns. So why hire a bookkeeper?

One reason for engaging a bookkeeper is cost. A bookkeeper may charge \$25 per month, or perhaps \$50 per calendar quarter. An accountant may charge \$75 per month, or per hour. (We are discussing services for a small studio or business operation. Larger business operations will undoubtedly cost more.)

Many photographers operating small businesses have asked for a simple bookkeeping method, so that they can maintain their own books. If you ask a bookkeeper or an accountant for such a system you may make enemies, not friends. A survey of several accountants may give you the feeling that you are dealing with a closed society, where most of the information is labeled "Top Secret," and inquisitive persons are not welcomed.

While preparing a seminar on business management, the author invited several accountants to participate. When they learned what information they would be expected to discuss, all refused to participate. One said he did not go to school to become a Certified Public Accountant (C.P.A.) in order to give information away free. (This was the same person who, when quoted the price for a photography project in a manufacturing company he owned, responded, "I can do it cheaper with my own camera.")

There are no laws at this time that compel us to engage bookkeepers or C.P.A.'s. If we can devise a method of keeping records that is understandable to ourselves, one that is simple, that we feel comfortable with, and one that tells us everything we have to know about our business, then that is the solution to our problem. When tax time rolls around we can extract the information needed by the person computing our tax returns.

A case in point. This was brought home to one photographer who had a C.P.A. set up his books and keep them up to date. He was charged a fee for the initial setting up, a monthly bookkeeping charge, and a quarterly accounting fee. The books were kept in the accountant's office and the business papers for each month were mailed in by the photographer. One month the photographer decided to see what he was paying for.

His request to see his books was met with the excuse that one of the bookkeepers was working on the records and that the following month would be a more opportune time. When he did get to see his books, he realized he did not know what he was looking at. The accountant explained that the records were set up according to certain accepted procedures and that he, the accountant, understood what was in the business ledger. The photographer asked the accountant to explain the ledger. He was willing to pay for the time. After the accountant had completed the explanation the photographer announced that he was taking his ledger home. "If I have to become a slave to an accountant, then it's time I learned how to keep my own ledger," he said.

We are not discussing a large business operation here. We are discussing a one- or two-person studio business. What the majority of small businesses need is a bookkeeping system that will serve two purposes: The proprietor can "go into" the ledger at any time for a reading on how good—or how poor—business is; and he can compare months or quarters of the current year with similar periods in previous years. He can of course turn the ledger over to his accountant at tax time or whenever required. A business ledger is like a road map, and unless the driver (business owner) can read the map (ledger) it is of no use to him.

There is no substitute for the convenience of having an accountant or a bookkeeper maintain your business records. The governing question is: Do you really need their services, or can you do it yourself?

A Basic Bookkeeping System

There are several ways in which you can set up your own bookkeeping system. Your accountant can do it for you, in which case you will then take over as your own bookkeeper. Or you can scout around, ask friends, read accounting books, and, finally, use trial and error. I suggest the first method as the best one. Even if you do your own tax returns, I recommend the services of an accountant in setting up the initial system. A professional can tell you what pitfalls to look out for, what should be listed where, which expenses are–and which are not–legitimately deductible. A C.P.A. will also save you time in hunting for the correct forms to use.

The illustrations shown in this chapter are for discussion only. These methods are not necessarily the best, nor are they the only ones that can be used. Any part can be changed to suit individual needs, or the entire discussion can be disregarded. Keep one thought in mind: There is no single system that will suit everyone's needs. The main purpose in presenting this chapter is to show the reader that simple methods of ledger keeping are possible if one wants to take the time to maintain his own records.

What Books Tell You

There are perhaps close to a hundred different ledger forms. Each has a purpose, or can be adapted to a purpose. In the beginning, unless you start with a system that has already been set up, you will have to use a trial-and-error method to find the form or forms that will suit your purpose. Ledger records can be kept on loose-leaf paper or in notebooks, but the standard forms available in stationery stores will generally result in a better working system. These come in several different sizes and with different ledger covers. The 11″ × 11″ size is popular and easy to handle.

A simple ledger can be divided into five sections: *Disbursements; Cash Received; Accounts Receivable; Balance Sheets* or *Cumulative Ledger; Accounts.*

Disbursements would show payments made by the business. *Cash Received* could also be *Receipts,* with all incoming monies recorded in this section. It is a register of your sales. *Accounts Receivable* shows what is outstanding and owed to you. Month-by-month or quarterly balances are shown in the *Balance Sheets* section. This is where you keep a running tab on your business. The section labeled *Accounts* is not required, but you may wish to add it to your ledger. This is where you can list your continuous accounts alphabetically. From the figures added up at the end of each month you have an immediate reading on how much business any particular account does. The total monthly figures can then be transferred into the *Accounts Receivable* section. The same figures can also be used to compare a client's month-by-month business in any one calendar year, or in comparative years. This is not a required section, but it is a handy one.

Determine your needs. In order to find out what types of forms are required for your purpose, it is best to do some preliminary groundwork. You know that two sections will be *Money In* and *Money Out.* Take a sheet of blank paper and list the numerous ways in which your business money flows in and out. You may have some, all, or more than the following: *Rent, Utilities, Wages, Insurance, Shipping, Repro/Printing, Darkroom, Film, Office Expenditures, Entertainment, Travel* and *Transportation, Professional Expenditures, Equipment, Equipment Maintenance.* A good catchall category is *Petty Cash,* which will be discussed in greater detail later on. Another two columns have to be provided for *Check Number* and the recipient–*Check To.* You must list every check that leaves your checkbook, including those that are voided for any reason. Under *Check To* you list the names to which the checks were made payable.

Adding all the requirements gives us a minimum of 16 items. In fact, if you send your processing to a professional lab *Processing* would make the seventeenth heading. That means that our ledger will have to have at least 17 columns, with one wide column for the name of the payee on the outgoing checks. You will find one form, a columnar type, that has 8 or 10 columns of equal width. You will also find that you may have to construct your ledger using different forms adjacent to each other–one form on the left side (as the book) lies open and a different form on the right side.

In this discussion we will be using Wilmer "Service" Line forms. The company has offices in North Hollywood, California. Each form has a code number between the top lines at the right. The accompanying figure shows Form 88-D. At the left is the *Record of Checks Drawn,* preprinted with all the necessary column headings: *Tax* information, a column for *Discounts, Check Amount, Check Number, Date,* name of the *Payee (In Favor of), Accounts Payable, Sundry Items.* The opposite side is *Distribution of Expenditures,* with ten columns. These columns can be used to show the amounts paid out for the items mentioned previously: *Utilities, Film, Office Expenditures,* etc.

Entering the Data

Let us assume that you have one column labeled *Telephone.* You write check #2555 to the Pacific Telephone Company in amount of $77.55. Under *Check Amount* you show $77.55. Going across, you enter the check number, the day of the month, and under *In Favor Of* you note "Pacific Telephone." Those are the entries on the left side of the ledger. On the right side of this two-page ledger, under *Telephone,* you show the amount, $77.55. Let us assume that the next item is rent. You would follow the same procedure. If you do not want to list utilities such as gas, electric, and telephone under separate column headings, then you would show them all under one column, *Utilities.* On the left side, under *Accounts Payable,* you can show what each amount went for: Gas, Water, Electric, etc. Remember that a commercially preprinted form is flexible. You can change it to suit your particular needs. Liquid blocking-out fluids are available at stationers in colors to match the color of your ledger sheets.

Why show amounts disbursed on both sides of the ledger? Let us assume you make substantial purchases from your photography supplier or camera store. Your month's bill is $450.38. If you show the amount of the check only, then you cannot break it down to: Film, $50.80; Processing, $235.75; Chemicals, $12.50; Equipment bag, $75.30; Tripod, $76.03. By showing only the total amount ($450.38) you have failed to accomplish two things: Your ledger does not show what your business uses in each category, and

Basic bookkeeping begins with basic data: "money in" and "money out" (on form 88-D).

NO. RECORD OF CHECKS DRAWN MONTH OF 1979 BANK

WILMER "SERVICE" LINE — STANDARD CHECK RECORD FORM 88-D

AMOUNT	ACCT.	FEDERAL	WITH-HOLDING	PETTY CASH	CHECK AMOUNT	√	CHECK NO.	DAY	IN FAVOR OF (CHECK TO)	ACCOUNTS PAYABLE	SUNDRY ITEMS ACCT.	SUNDRY ITEMS AMOUNT	√
									AMOUNTS FORWARDED				
									January				
					2 22		1330	5	Sun Rubber Stamp				
					345 27		1331	6	F. X. Sales				
					98 60		1332	6	Bell Telephone				
					23 10		1333	6	Stationers, Inc				
					783 93		1334	17	Photo Equipment Co.				
					15 00		1335	22	Postmaster				
					3 82		1336	22	United Parcel Service				
							1337	—	Void				
					450 00		1338	29	Realty Corp, Inc				
					75 15		1339	30	Water + Power				
				8 50				30					
				8 50	1797 09								
				(+ 8.50) =	1805 59								
									February				
					74 37		1340	2	Hi Photo Supplies				
					85 00		1341	2	Prof. Photog. Assn		DUES	85 00	
					327.97		1342	3	Health Plan Co.		Health Insur	327 97	
					92 21		1343	4	Bell Telephone				
					75 18		1344	4	American Express				
					18 08		1345	7	Xerox Repro				
					2 10		1346	15	United Parcel				
					122 57		1347	18	Album Corp				
					19 20		1348	25	Center Focus Sales				
					210 09		1349	25	F. X. Sales				
					450 00		1350	27	Realty Corp, Inc.				
1500	Draw				1500 00		1351	28	Jack B.				
				10 19				28					
1500 00				10 19								412 97	
				(+10.19) =	2986 96								

The numbers over the detailed headings are explained in the text on page 88.

DISTRIBUTION OF EXPENDITURES MONTH OF 19 NO.

WILMER SERVICE LINE STANDARD CHECK RECORD FORM 88-D

	#101 UTILITIES	#102 RENT	#103 FILM	#104 PROCESSING	#105 OFFICE SUPPLIES	#106 TELEPHONE	#107 TRAVEL ENTERTAINMENT	#108 EQUIPMENT #109 SERVICE	#110 SHIPPING POSTAGE	#111 PHOTO SUPPLIES
1										
2					2 22					
3				345 27						
4						98 60				
5					23 10					
6								#108 183 93		
7									15 00	
8									3 82	
9										
10		450 00								
11	75 15									
12					8 50					
13										
14							781			
15	75 15	450 00		345 27	33 82	98 60	MILES	183 93	18 82	
16										
17										
18			52 27	22 10						
19										
20										
21						92 21				
22							75 18			
23					18 08					
24									2 10	
25										122 57
26				19 20						
27				210 09						
28		450 00								
29										
30					9 89	30				
31										
32		450 00	52 27	251 39	27 97	92 51	75 18		2 10	122 57
33							990 MILES			
34										
35										
36										
37										
38										
39										
40										

you have not abided by the law regarding expenditures for equipment.

You cannot deduct the total amount paid for equipment at one time but should depreciate it over a period—approximately five years is usual. Therefore you have to itemize each expenditure group and then, at the end of your fiscal year, either you or your accountant can "go into the books," pick up the amounts spent for equipment, and depreciate those figures over the acceptable time period. These amounts must be carried over into following years to complete the computation cycle. That is why you show the total amount of the check on one side of the ledger and the item-by-item breakdown on the other side.

Monthly sums. At the end of the month you draw a line under the last entry and add up each of the columns. If everything has been paid by check, then the totals of all the columns added together should equal the total of all the checks.

Petty cash. Many businesses find a Petty Cash account useful. Let us assume you have photocopies of several letters made. The total amount is 12 cents. It will probably cost you more to write a check for that amount (in check charges and service fees) than the face amount of the check. Therefore it would be better to pay cash, get a dated receipt, and mark it with the type of expenditure: Photocopy. Instead of having a corresponding check number for this item you would mark a column on the left side of the ledger with the notation *Petty Cash* and note 12 cents. That same amount is marked on the right side of the ledger under the appropriate heading. You may decide that the amounts spent on a daily basis are too small for individual entries. You can save these up until the end of the month and show the total as one entry, with a notation that it represents the whole month's tally. Some larger businesses require a Petty Cash voucher, or written record, for each item. In a small business this is really a waste of time and money. It is different in an operation involving many employees, where a check on petty-cash outflow is needed. In a small or one-person studio operation, a slip of paper with continuous entries for outgo can be kept in the petty-cash box. Then, at the end of the month, that paper is dated, totaled, and included in the monthly accounting. If you start the Petty Cash box with $50, then your outgo total plus the amount left should equal $50. If it does not, then either someone is "tapping" the Petty Cash box or you are not keeping your tally sheet accurately enough.

Car expense. What do you do with automobile expenses? If the car is leased by the business, then the lease payments take care of part of the problem. Your gasoline purchases should be charged, and paid for by check, as well as the yearly license fees and any other expenses associated with operation of the vehicle for your business.

If your automobile is used for both business and personal use, that is a different matter. And if the car is registered in your name and not in a company name, then accounting is a litttle different again.

A privately owned vehicle that is used for business can be compensated for in different ways. There is a figure the Internal Revenue Service allows for this purpose. The government figure—about 18 cents per mile for 1979—is based on what it costs to operate the *average* motor vehicle. You must use the approved figure and also account for every mile you drive for business purposes. Incidentally, the per-mile figure is supposed to include such overhead items as insurance, replacement of tires, batteries, gasoline, etc.

If you use the per-mile figure for automobile expense deductions, then you must keep a running account of the mileage. A good place to start is with a daily calendar with spaces for notations. The Robinson "File-Away" #C35-12/315, -12/330, is handy for this purpose as well as for daily appointments. It is a 16½″ × 20″ wall calendar. At the end of each day you mark down the number of business miles traveled. You can even circle the number to make it stand out.

Going back to the ledger, you can either enter the mileage on a daily basis, taking one of the columns for this purpose, or you can enter it as a monthly figure. (Although the I.R.S. would like to see a daily itemized listing, they will accept a total figure if you have kept a record of the daily figures somewhere—such as on the calendar. The wall calendar can be rolled up at the end of the year and filed with the other business papers.) At the end of every month, take the total mileage for that month, multiply it by the allowance factor, and enter the dollar amount in the ledger as an expense. That covers the use of the automobile.

Now you have all your expenses listed in one section of your business ledger. If you need more columns on the right side, you can either add another Form 88-D or use Form 97-C, which is also for *distribution.* It is up to you, the record keeper, to utilize the available business forms to your own best advantage. Stores that carry these supplies have illustrated catalogues. Spend some time familiarizing yourself with the forms and make your decisions carefully. The forms you choose should make your work easier, not more complicated.

Using Coded Headings

Some accountants like to use code figures for the column headings, or in conjunction with them. Thus, you may find a heading such as *Processing* #104, or simply #104. This number is then keyed to a master layout where each type of expenditure is assigned a number: *Utilities* #101, *Rent* #102, *Film* #103, *Processing* #104, *Office Supplies* #105, etc. Then whenever you see the number #103 in the ledger you will know that it means film. (If the columns have word headings, then a master list is not required.) If you are working with an accountant, he will set the system up for you. If you are doing it alone, then use the system that is easiest for you. If, at tax time, you have to go back into the heart of your books in order to pull out specific items, then you must have a key that keeps the system simple.

How to Record Income

The next part of the ledger is *Cash Received.* This is where you show payments made to the business. You can also show bank deposits on these ledger pages. The central column of the Wilmer Form 62-D shown here is headed *Received From.* The other columns can be headed as follows: *Sales Taxes Collected, Invoice Number, No Tax (Out of State). Net Amount Received* and *Day* are already preprinted on the form. Both sides of this form are alike.

The record of income has a separate column for sales taxes collected (form 62- D).

3/4

RECORD OF CASH RECEIVED MONTH OF 19 79 NO.

WILMER ★ SERVICE LINE — STANDARD CASH RECEIVED FORM 62-D

Bank Deposits Date	Bank Deposits Amount	Sales Tax Rcd	Net Amount Received	Day	Received From	Total Invoice Amt	General Ledger Cr. Acct.	General Ledger Cr. Amount
					AMOUNTS FORWARDED			
					January			
		2.97	49.50	3	Williams #83125	52.47		
		45.00	750.00	3	Jackson #83126	795.00		
4	1097.32	14.14	235.71	4	Franklin #83127	249.85		
6	540.87	30.62	510.25	6	Gold #83128	540.87		
		7.50	125.00	10	Matthews #83129	132.50		
14	2453.25	131.36	2189.39	14	O'Donnell & Co	2320.75	2525C	
15	556.15	31.50	525.00	15	B. Mfg Co.	556.15	2710C	
16	132.50	7.50	125.00	16	N.H. Ltd	132.50	2438 L	
20	24.54	1.39	23.15	20	Arrowhead #83130	24.54		
27	397.71	22.51	375.20	27	J. B. Nelson #83131	397.71		
	5202.34	294.14	4908.20			5202.34		
					February			
		4.50	75.00	2	Baker #83132	79.50		
		7.13	118.75	2	Ellis #83133	125.88		
3	1038.80	58.80	980.00	3	Roscoe #83134	1038.80		
		4.35	72.50	4	Hillside Co. #83135	76.85		
4	811.96	41.61	693.50	4	Pre-Rule Co. Inc.	735.11	2515 C	
7	1166.53	66.03	1100.50	7	Mar-White Assoc.	1166.53	2272 C	
8	2413.62	136.62	2277.00	8	True Fruit	2413.62	2110 C	
10	37.47	2.12	35.35	10	Martin #83136	37.47		
15	583.00	33.00	550.00	15	Cassidy & Assoc	583.00	2233 L	
		8.70	145.00	18	Gerrard #83137	153.70		
19	819.12	37.67	627.75	19	Paley #83138	665.42		
		5.62	93.60	21	Ernest #83139	99.22		
		91.55	1525.75	22	Straight Rule Co.	1617.30	2517 C	
		19.65	327.50	22	Allen #83140	347.15		
22	2886.18	46.56	775.95	22	Tate #83141	822.51		
		16.24	270.70	25	Hale #83142	286.94		
		27.02	450.25	27	C.B. Gross Co. #83143	477.27		
28	810.59	2.63	43.75	28	Sherman #83144	46.38		
	10772.65	609.80	10162.85			10772.65		

Accounts receivable records are simplified by this form, 44-C.

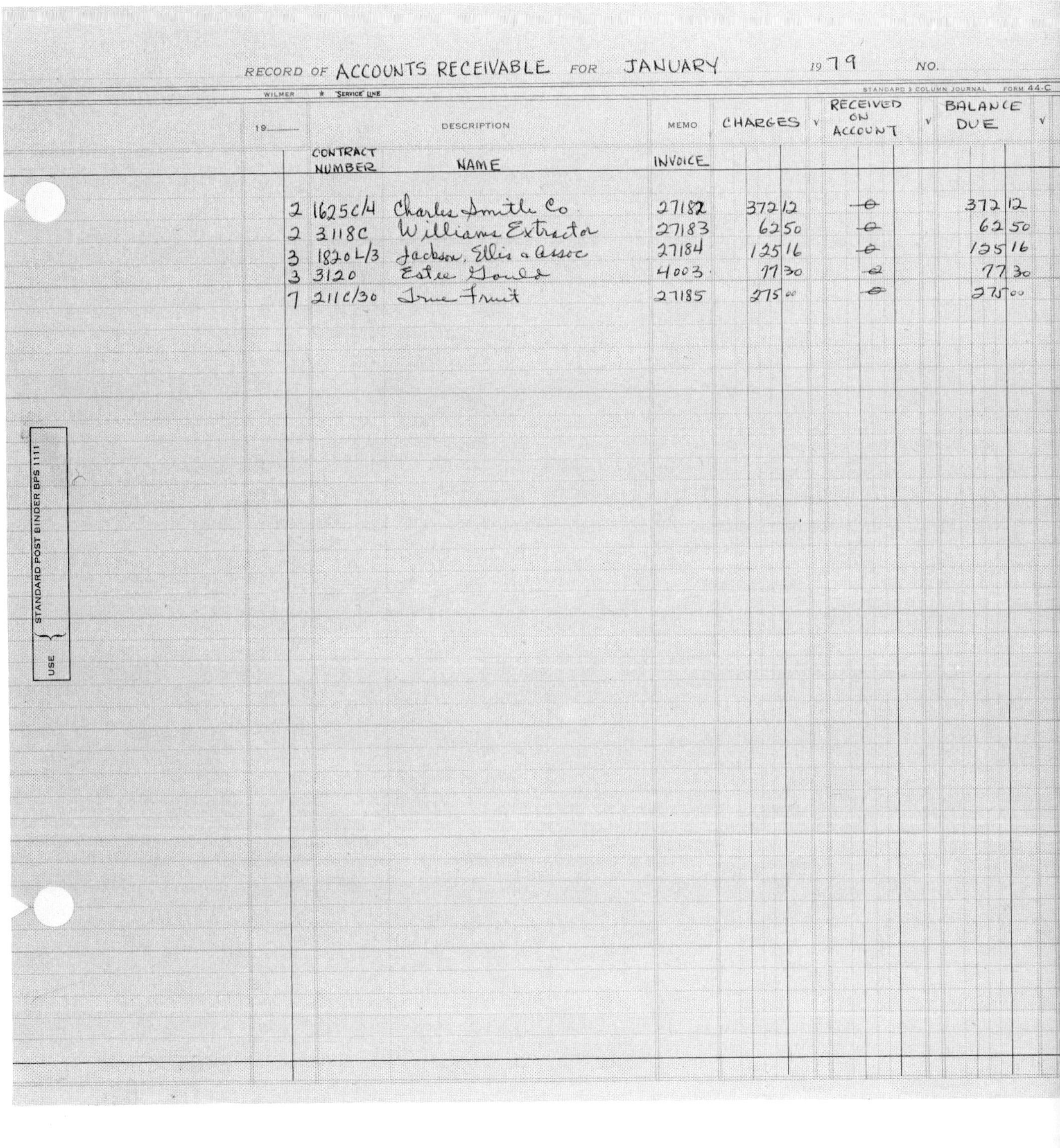

RECORD OF ACCOUNTS RECEIVABLE FOR JANUARY 1979 NO.

WILMER ★ "SERVICE" LINE — STANDARD 3 COLUMN JOURNAL FORM 44-C

19__	DESCRIPTION: CONTRACT NUMBER	DESCRIPTION: NAME	MEMO: INVOICE	CHARGES	√	RECEIVED ON ACCOUNT	√	BALANCE DUE	√
2	1625C/4	Charles Smith Co	27182	372 12		–0–		372 12	
2	3118C	Williams Extractor	27183	62 50		–0–		62 50	
3	1820L/3	Jackson, Ellis & Assoc	27184	125 16		–0–		125 16	
3	3120	Estee Gould	4003	77 30		–0–		77 30	
7	211C/30	True Fruit	27185	275 00		–0–		275 00	

USE { STANDARD POST BINDER BPS 1111

If all the receipts are deposited in the bank at the end of the business day, then that figure can be noted in a column labeled *Bank Deposits.* If you want to have a closer breakdown of where the income came from, such as *Photography, Frames, Albums,* etc., then use Form 62-D on the left side and a columnar form containing perhaps eight or ten columns on the right side when your ledger book is opened flat. In that way you can total up both sides of the ledger and balance one against the other, as was done with *Disbursements.*

The *Accounts Receivable* section tells what is due from whom, when. Wilmer's Standard Three-Column Journal Form 44-C can be used for this purpose. There is room for the date the charges were incurred, the account number and name, the invoice number, and current charges, as well as the balance forward and total amount due. The small space after each column can be used to indicate how long a balance has been in effect: If more than 30 days, insert "30d" after the dollar amount; if part of it is 30 days old and another part is 60 days, then this can also be noted. (Chapter 21 will have some suggestions about collecting from slow payers.)

What you are doing is organizing your business dealings into an efficient record. That is really what bookkeeping is all about. You can't keep records on nondescript pieces of paper and then expect to be able to fill out your tax forms at the end of the year with any degree of accuracy. Nor can you expect to be able to answer questions intelligently if the Internal Revenue Service should decide to audit your tax return.

How to See Where You Stand

Balance sheets can also be called *cumulative ledgers* and can be maintained in many ways. As previously stated, some people like a "running" cumulative accounting, while others prefer a simple record.

In the running cumulative method you add the current figures beside the previously posted ones and then total the two amounts. In this way you have a cumulative accounting for every business item. If film expenses were $75 in January and $98.35 in February,

The cumulative ledger on form 97-C (see pages 91 and 94) shows your monthly expenditures.

DISTRIBUTION OF ITEMS CUMULATIVE LEDGER FOR DISBURSEMENTS 1979 NO.

WILMER ★ "SERVICE" LINE — STANDARD 16 COLUMN DISTRIBUTION FORM 97-C

		ENTERTAINMENT	MILEAGE	EQUIPMENT	SERVICE	SHIPPING	POSTAGE	PHOTO SUPPLIES	TRAVEL EXPENSES	SUNDRY ITEMS: INSURANCE	SUNDRY ITEMS: MISC.
		A/C #107		A/C #108	A/C #109	A/C # 110		A/C #111	A/C 112		
JANUARY	1		7 81	783 93		3 82	15 00				
FEBRUARY	2	75 18	9 90			2 10		122 57		327 97	85 00
MARCH	3		13 21		75 27	7 85	1 55	173 20			
APRIL	4	98 47	11 87			5 35	15 00	80 10			
MAY	5	62 50	10 05			10 70				327 97	
JUNE	6	258 80	10 97		90 30	6 36		25 20	407 32		
	7										
	8										
	9										
	10										
	11										
	12										
	13										
	14										
	15										
	16										
	17										
	18										
	19										
	20										
	21										
	22										
	23										
	24										
	25										
	26										
	27										
	28										
	29										
	30										
	31										
	32										
	33										
	34										
	35										
	36										
	37										
	38										
	39										
	40										

USE { STANDARD POST BINDER BPS 1111 / DELUXE POST BINDER BPD 1111 }

The cumulative ledger on form 44-C keeps track of what you are taking in.

RECORD OF CUMULATIVE LEDGER FOR CASH RECEIVED 19 79 NO.

WILMER ★ "SERVICE" LINE — STANDARD 3 COLUMN JOURNAL FORM 44-C

19___	DESCRIPTION	MEMO	TOTAL SALES		√	SALES TAXES RECEIVED		√	NET SALES		√
	JANUARY		5202	34		294	14		4908	20	
	FEBRUARY		10772	65		609	80		10162	85	
	MARCH		16806	41		951	31		15855	10	
	APRIL		9563	00		541	30		9021	70	
	MAY		12265	13		694	25		11570	88	
	JUNE										
	JULY										
	AUGUST										
	SEPTEMBER										
	OCTOBER										
	NOVEMBER										
	DECEMBER										

USE { STANDARD POST BINDER BPS 1111

$40.70 in March, $95.25 in April, $117.90 in May, $373.75 in June, $255.35 in July, etc., you would have a double entry for every month except January. For example, the February entry would show $98.35 for that month and $173.35 for *Expenditures to Date.* The July entry would show $255.35 for that month and $1056.30 as the cumulative amount from January up to and including the month of July.

The running cumulative system takes a lot of room, needing two columns for every item. The simpler method is to show single monthly entries for each item, as shown in the accompanying illustrations. Form 97-C is used for *Disbursements* and Form 44-C is used for *Cash Received.*

In legal photography, the basic client is the lawyer or the insurance company who needs the pictures. These commercial accounts are like other commercial clients in that they will pay 60 days, 90 days, or even six months after the initial billing date, and so you will need a system for keeping tabs on the account. Wilmer's *Accounts Receivable* Form 5-D is ideal for this purpose (see illustration). The attorney's name is entered at the top of the page, and the preprinted columns are used as designated: *Date, Description, Posting Ref., Charges, Credits, Balance.*

Under *Description,* write the name of the subject that you photographed at the lawyer's request. Under *Posting Reference* add the contract or file number you assigned to the lawyer, followed by the job number you gave to this particular assignment, as explained in detail in the chapter on filing systems. When you receive payment for some, or all, of the invoiced items, enter the credit in the corresponding column on the next available line and cross-reference the payment to the accounts concerned. Now you have a running cumulative accounting of your dealings with this client. A sample Form 5-D as used for a commercial client, True Fruit, is included for comparison. Whenever any account lags too far behind in payment, it is a simple matter to photocopy the ledger page with the information and send it to the client with a request for payment.

Taking all this accounting, or bookkeeping, into consideration, what do you have with this system? You have a system. That is a simple fact. How good is

Form 5-D has room to list the assignment for commercial clients.

ACCOUNTS

SHEET NO. NAME TRUE FRUIT (ACCT. #2110 C.)

CREDIT RATING CREDIT LIMIT ADDRESS

WILMER ★ "SERVICE" LINE STANDARD BALANCE LEDGER FORM 5-D

	19 79	DESCRIPTION	POSTING REF.	CHARGES	√	CREDITS	√	BALANCE	√	DR. OR CR.
January			2110 C/							
	5	Location - Beach	30	275 00				275 00		
	7	Studio - Point of Purchase	31	650 80				925 80		
	15	Studio - Small Products	32	315 80				1240 80		
	20	Studio - Display	33	472 82				1713 62		
	25	Studio - Misc. Items	34	250 20				1963 82		
	26	Location - Market	35	449 80				2413 62		
		January Balance						2413 62		
February		Amount Forward		2413 62						
	3	Location - Market		750 90		-0-		3164 52		
	5	Studio - Display		125 88				3290 40		
	9	Studio - Point of Purchase		650 80				3941 20		
	12					2413 62		1527 52		
	18	Studio - Point of Purchase		1865 20				3392 78		
	27	Studio - Market Display		565 80				3958 58		

USE { STANDARD POST BINDER BPS 1111 / DELUXE POST BINDER BPD 1111

Legal clients, too, need space in the ledger for details.

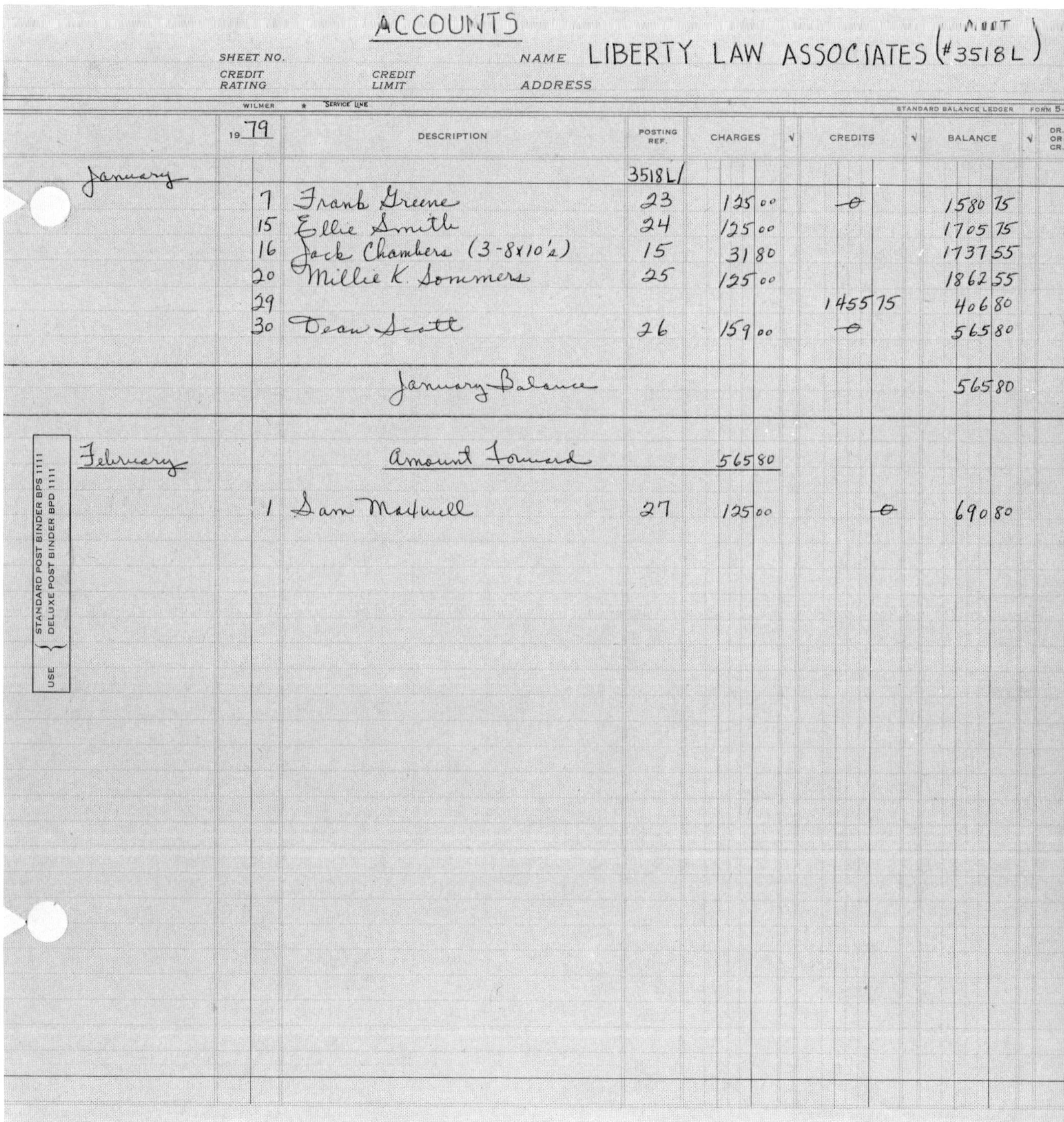

ACCOUNTS

SHEET NO. NAME LIBERTY LAW ASSOCIATES (ACCT #3518L)

CREDIT RATING CREDIT LIMIT ADDRESS

WILMER ★ SERVICE LINE STANDARD BALANCE LEDGER FORM 5-D

19 79		DESCRIPTION	POSTING REF.	CHARGES	√	CREDITS	√	BALANCE	√	DR. OR CR.
January			3518L/							
	7	Frank Greene	23	125 00		-0-		1580 75		
	15	Ellie Smith	24	125 00				1705 75		
	16	Jack Chambers (3-8x10's)	15	31 80				1737 55		
	20	Millie K. Sommers	25	125 00				1862 55		
	29					1455 75		406 80		
	30	Dean Scott	26	159 00		-0-		565 80		
		January Balance						565 80		
February		Amount Forward		565 80						
	1	Sam Maxwell	27	125 00		-0-		690 80		

USE { STANDARD POST BINDER BPS 1111 / DELUXE POST BINDER BPD 1111 this system? Just as good as any other system—if it works for you. If it doesn't work, then it is just as bad as any other system that doesn't work. Every professional bookkeeper, every certified accountant, every private person keeping a record or a file has a pet system for accomplishing recordkeeping. Each one uses the system he or she feels comfortable with.

If you listen to the accountant's tale, his work is very complex. To a certain extent that may be true, but education, training, and experience will help a person to understand and master accountkeeping. Actually, there are fewer mysteries in accounting than there are in the mechanics of photography.

Studios and Leases

CHAPTER 10

In order to decide whether or not to have a studio, we must first know what is meant by a *studio.*

Is a photography business in a store considered a studio? Is a photography business carried on in a private residence a studio? What are the qualifying marks?

Store studios were operational bases for portrait and wedding photographers in the 1920s, 1930s, and 1940s. Today many successful wedding and portrait photographers operate out of their homes. There are also many photographic businesses in office-building suites. In New York City numerous established photographers have studios in disused factory loft buildings. Elsewhere there are studios in houses that have been converted completely from homes to commercial enterprise.

Locating Your Studio

The item of importance to any business is customer contact. Where a particular type of photographic enterprise is located for maximum benefit to that business, is of prime concern. A studio in a house close to Century City, a prestigious commercial and residential complex in Southern California, would probably not be as successful as a studio located right in the mall. The exposure afforded by the central location would be the prime factor in generating business. On the other hand, fashion photographers, industrial, commercial, or public relations photographers would probably do as well in an office-building suite as they would in a store-front studio: They are not dependent upon pedestrian trade.

Let us consider the store-front studio, keeping in mind that many of the points discussed will also apply to studios in homes and office buildings.

The first thing a customer sees is the display window or a showcase. The photographs must be current, clean, and representative of the photographer's best work. As photographers, we know that color prints fade. We also know that fading is fastest when sunlight or fluorescent light strikes the photographs. This means that studio displays in shopping malls fade even if they are in an inside location where there is no sunlight—the fluorescent lights have the same long-term effect. The photographs in display windows should be changed every three months if feasible, every six months at the least. Every three or six months photographs can be rotated to an inside wall and new pictures put up outside. The idea is to make it seem that your photographs are continually being changed. The customer who shops in your area must be attracted to your window or display cases. If you do nothing to attract attention, people will simply pass your studio without realizing it exists. Constantly changing photographs can be good attention getters.

Planning the Interior

Is the interior of your studio attractive and inviting? I have seen some that looked like barns. The primary purpose of the reception room is to make the prospective customer feel comfortable. Do you have enough seating accommodation? One studio, which has long since gone out of business, specialized in school photography. As a result of the high-school business, their wedding photography was plentiful. However, when a prospective bride and her parents came in to inquire about wedding photography anyone else entering the studio had to either stand or sit on the floor. No thought was given to customer comfort and convenience. This is where the second impression is made upon the prospective customer.

Basically, the reception room should not be the place where business matters are discussed. You certainly do not want conversations with clients to be overheard. Business negotiations are private matters and should be conducted in a room, or an area, away from the main reception area. Proofs or previews should not be discussed in the main reception room, either. What is needed is several areas where clients can feel they are given complete privacy. Mrs. Smith doesn't want everyone in the reception area to know that her husband works for XXX Company, that she lives at 222222 Main Street, and that her telephone number is 555-1212. She doesn't like others to know that her daughter's wedding photography at $500 is more than she wanted to spend, that she desires a less expensive package, and that she still wants a nice album of photographs. Some thoughtless salesperson might ask, "Do you want a cheaper package?" and Mrs. Smith's face would probably turn crimson. Mrs. Smith doesn't want a "cheaper package." Mrs. Smith wants a *less expensive* package. And Mrs. Smith does not want to broadcast the details of the transaction. She desires privacy.

While on the matter of privacy, a source of customer irritation is constant interruptions distracting the studio representative with whom the customer is discussing business matters. I have seen many persons become irritated when interruptions reached the point of straining patience, with the end result of a lost customer.

The telephone is a good example of an instrument that can ring up "No Sale" if it is not handled judiciously. The customer does not care to sit idly by while you discuss some other client's business or—especially—your private social arrangements. The customer expects your undivided attention.

Added Comforts

There is nothing wrong with having soft music playing in the reception area, and there is nothing wrong in having refreshments available. Coffee, tea, cookies, and soft drinks can sometimes make the difference in how the customer reacts to your sales pitch. Restroom facilities are also important. In an actual case, a prospective client was in the studio with a four-year-old child. The youngster needed the facilities of a restroom, but the photographer insisted there was none on the premises. It wasn't funny when the youngster couldn't restrain himself any longer. The mother picked up her child and left. Her parting words were, "Call me when you have a restroom." There was a restroom on the premises, but it was closed to all except studio personnel. The owner said he was tired of cleaning up the messes customers left in the restroom, he did not like having to repaint the restroom walls after six months of graffiti collecting, and he was not in the sanitation business. While it may be a fact that many retail establishments keep their restrooms closed to the general public, it is a common basic fact of life that human needs must be accommodated.

If you do a lot of family photography and child photography, there should be an area where toys and games are available. Youngsters have low patience thresholds, and their impatience can sometimes thwart a sale. Get them away from the parent, in a supervised area where they can play while the parent shops, and you have things going in your favor.

A point to keep in mind is that, even with the best arrangements, very young children can wet themselves and need a change of garments. Parents sometimes prepare for these emergencies by carrying extra diapers for babies, but sometimes they forget to prepare for emergencies with older children. Pants, underpants, and socks, as well as disposable diapers, should be stocked in a studio that does a lot of child photography. Ask your attorney about your liability if someone uses one or more of such items supplied by the studio, as garments may not be reusable. It is best to check with your local health department or other government agency that has jurisdiction over such matters in your area.

Adapt to Different Specialties

The *commercial studio* has a different clientele. The individual customer conference room may not be necessary, yet many of the conditions that apply to portrait studios also apply here. Fashion photographers interviewed recently pointed out that music was used in the studio to help the model work more easily. Music can be used in the portrait studio, as well. And the commercial photography studio should not be any less attractive than the portrait studio.

In *legal photography* an office-studio combination is sometimes all that is needed. Most of the shooting is done on location. For the one percent or so of the work that is done in the studio, small accommodations will suffice.

The office doesn't have to be outfitted with photographs of people with cuts, bruises, open wounds, and gruesome scars. Indeed, it should have some nice scenic photographs of landscapes, seascapes, aerial views of mountains, and so on. After all, you are a photographer. What better way to decorate the walls of your office and studio than with beautiful photographs?

An atmosphere of comfort and cordiality will do more towards increasing sales than all your sales literature. Regardless of the type of photography you specialize in, make your facilities inviting, and the rewards will be worth the investment.

The Business Lease

Reading every word in a contract is of prime importance. It is equally important that you understand fully the meaning of each part of the contract *before* you affix your signature to the document. If you pay, what do you receive? If you do not pay, what happens? What do you stand to lose?

The lease for a photographer's place of business is a contract. It specifies what must be paid to the owner of the premises, the form or schedule of payments, the type of lease, the length of time the contract will be in effect, options to renew, subleasing, what services the rental fees cover, and security deposits, if applicable. These are a few of the items that can be covered in a lease agreement.

A good business person will not sign a lease without the advice or assistance of an attorney. The property owners want to protect their interests, and will do this with the lease agreement. The person leasing the property must also protect his or her interests. One case in point is that of the shopping-mall complex. If you were to lease space for a photography studio, you would want to be certain that no other photographic establishments operated in the same complex—you want no built-in competition.

How Long a Lease?

Let's assume you want to purchase an existing studio and that the lease has eight months to go before expiration. In business operations, an eight-month lease is nothing. Just as you are getting acquainted with the business operation you will be faced with renewal negotiations. What would you do if the current monthly rent of $500 is raised to $750 or $1000?

Many businesses, when faced with selling, will attempt to renegotiate with the owner(s) of the property. If an eight-month lease of the premises can be extended to two years or five years, the chance of a sale of the business will be better. Although an option to renew could serve the same purpose, the option might be written at a higher rental. Renegotiation can be a harrowing experience at any time. What if you are faced with an increase in rent and your business income does not warrant paying that increase? All your investment will go down the drain if you vacate the premises; but there is nothing else you can do in view of the fact that you cannot afford the additional payment. So here you are, eight months after buying the business, faced with the realities of life: Money is the bottom line.

Leasing Variables

A long lease with a sublet option is desirable. If you find that for any reason you do not wish to remain in that location, the sublet clause works to your advantage. In fact, you can probably make money in the process. In subleasing, the third party makes the payments to you and you, in turn, make the required payments to the owner. If you sublet at a figure that is more than your contractual obligation, then you are making a profit on the deal.

A lease for two years with a renewal option may be acceptable. Everything depends upon the renewal option. What is the rental fee upon renewal? How long will the lease be renewed for? Is the renewal clause, or option, applicable to new tenants in case of a sale of the business, or only to the original occupant? Will the lease keep running on a month-to-month basis upon expiration?

Month-to-month rental is actually no lease at all. The tenant can be notified to vacate the premises upon the properly stipulated notice, which is usually a written notification. You cannot enter into any long-term advertising campaigns because you really do not know how long you will be at that location. If you are paying $500 per month and someone offers the owner $750, you will find yourself out of that place unless you can counter that offer. You are on a perpetual springboard. The property owner can keep raising your rent by simply telling you that he has received a better offer for the premises. You then have to either put up or move.

A good question is: What happens in the case of a long lease when the business is not going well and the owner may have to close up? There really isn't much that the property owners can do to the tenant if the business is registered as a corporation. The corporation can file for bankruptcy. The property owner does not benefit by instituting legal proceedings against a defunct corporation with no tangible assets. The owners can file and become one of the creditors to be paid—if there are ever any assets; but none of the personal assets of corporate officers or stockholders can be seized to satisfy any debts incurred by the now-bankrupt organization.

If the business is listed as individually owned or as a partnership, then the persons named as owners are personally liable for the remaining term of the lease. In these cases it is advisable to discuss the situation with the owner or owners. If general business conditions in that area are good, you might be released from the rental contract with perhaps only the loss of a payment of an additional month's rent—or none at all. Or you could try to sublet the property, if this is permitted in your lease document. If the tenant does not reach an agreement with the landlord, then the landlord, or property owner, can institute legal proceedings to seize the personal assets of the signers of the lease.

A lawyer should inspect and approve your business lease and all contracts before you sign the documents. Throughout your business career you will find that your attorney can be your best friend.

CHAPTER 11

The Professional Photographer

What is a *professional photographer*? How does the *professional* photographer differ from the *freelance* photographer? and the *part-timer* or the *weekender*? We may say, correctly, that a person who works at one principal calling is a professional. While a studio-owner–photographer and his employee–photographers can be classified as professionals, so can those who operate out of their homes or from offices. As long as photography is the main calling, or vocation, the photographer can be classed with the professionals.

The true amateur is one who pursues the art as a pastime rather than as a profession. *Freelance* denotes a person who is not tied to a specific base. A freelance photographer can sell services to another photographer or to a studio owner on a contractual basis from job to job, or can act independently. Even without benefit of a studio, however, the freelancer whose chief source of income is photography is a professional photographer.

Then there are the news photographer and the magazine or newspaper staff *photojournalist*, to whom photography is a livelihood.

The *weekender* and the *part-timer* are the ones who use photography as an avocation, not a vocation. They may be employed regularly in some profession or trade, from medicine to truck driving. Even though they engage in photography for hire in their off-hours they are not *professional* photographers.

Some professional photography organizations may say that any person who has a city business permit and/or a state Resale Certificate, and who has published a notice of doing business, is, by all intent, a professional photographer. By all intent, yes. By the definition found in the dictionary, no. Photography may be an art form, but it is also big business. It is an integral part of our business world, our teaching and educational processes, and our leisure activities. Today's photographer should be educated in the science of photography—and also in the business of photography. The general public, too, must be educated. The public must be made aware of the difference between a professional and a nonprofessional.

Being a professional photographer is different from simply *calling* yourself one. It is more than being a member of a photography association and displaying the association's symbols.

The difference between a professional and a nonprofessional, as defined in a dictionary on the basis of source of income, has already been stated. Let us add some modifiers to that definition.

- The professional should act like a professional.
- A person who is a professional in his or her calling shows this professionalism in part by dress, grooming, personal mannerisms, speech, and conduct in relations with other persons.
- Professionalism is an entire concept, the sum total of individual items.

CHAPTER 12 Personnel

Personnel has a greater impact upon business operations than many persons believe—including the employees who make up the personnel. As an example, let us take the case of a truck driver on the street or highway. If the driving manners of the person in the vehicle are obnoxious, and if the firm's name is emblazoned on the vehicle, then you can be sure that the next time you need a plumber, carpenter, or whatever the service offered by the company, you would not call that particular firm. Employees are the front line of contact between the company and potential clients. I don't know the president of my bank on a personal basis, but I do know the tellers and officers of the branch at which I do my banking. As far as I am concerned, they are the bank. And that is true for department stores, service companies, and retail merchants.

Keep in mind the example of the bank president when you hire employees, especially other photographers. Although the contracting parties may have met you during contract negotiations, it is your employees they will be in contact with in 99 percent of their business association with your company. And the guests at the event probably do not know you at all. They see the photographer, and the photographer becomes "John Doe Studio" in their minds. It is this impression that makes the difference between future sales and future "No Sale."

If your receptionist answers the telephone as though she is in a hurry at all times, then something had better be done. If she is continuously rushed, then she obviously needs assistance. Perhaps she has too much work. The telephone is sometimes the first line of contact between the customer and the studio. (More about this in the next chapter.) The conversation should be short but inviting—inviting the caller to visit the studio, where your works are displayed and sales resistance is lowest.

One photographer had the idea that a busy phone indicated a busy photographer. Whenever he left the studio Photographer Busy would take the telephone off the hook. This would cause a busy signal to be received by anyone calling the studio.

"Why do you do that?" I asked.

"Well, when people get the busy signal they think this is a busy place. That makes them want me to do the photography for them. After all, if I'm so busy, then I must be good."

"Wouldn't they get tired of hearing the busy signal and call a not-so-busy photographer?" I asked.

"No, I think I have the right idea," he replied.

Well, about three months later the store had a "For Rent" sign in the window. He "busied" himself out of business. The man was trying to impress customers with the wrong tactics.

The person answering the studio telephone should be courteous, should keep calls brief, and should not make the caller wish that another studio had been called. It never pays to be short with anyone. Every inquiry is a potential customer, at one time or another. More about this later.

Looking Good

Grooming and dress are important for everyone. While we, as individuals, can walk around in our own homes in any state of dress or undress, wearing any kind of garments we desire, with our hair in any arrangement, we do not do so in the business world. Here we are governed by certain codes, specified by our employers, our customers, our business associates.

The photographer at a wedding should not dress in such a way as to be conspicuous among the guests. A male does not necessarily wear a tuxedo or a tailcoat to a formal affair. In a simple black suit, with white shirt and a gray or black tie, he would blend very nicely with the assembled guests. It would be ludicrous for him to show up in sports clothes. The same applies to a female photographer. She does not have to wear an evening gown, but her clothes should not stand out like a red carnation in a group of gardenias. Discretion and subtlety are the bywords.

The same is true in the office and the studio, where service personnel should dress as the occasion dictates.

Personal grooming is also very important in and out of the studio. Dirty hair, unkempt fingernails, torn or dirty clothing, and body odor have no place in the business world, any more than tight see-through blouses and short skirts. This is especially true in photography, where personal contact is so much a part of the business.

Conduct on the job is another important item. One company has a set of rules for its photographers to follow. Those that do not are told to look for jobs elsewhere. The rules state that there are to be

- no consumption of liquor at a social function, even if invited by the host(s) or guests;
- no smoking on the job;
- no fraternizing with guests;
- no friends to be invited, either to keep you company or to act as your assistant;
- no distribution of any business cards other than the studio's own;
- no solicitation for more work.

The rules work. They are enforced to the extent that several talented photographers were fired for breaking one or more of those rules. On one assignment the photographer brought his girl friend along. When the supervisor entered the reception room, the photographer and friend were in a corner, sipping drinks. The photographer's explanation that they were going to a party after the event was over did not go down too well with the supervisor. The picture possibilities—such as grandparents dancing with their great-grandchildren—did not mean anything to the preoccupied photographer. The supervisor asked for all the exposed film, dismissed the photographer, and proceeded to shoot the event as it should have been done: with undivided attention.

Fringe Benefits

Fringe benefits apply to employers as well as to employees. These may take the form of medical and hospital insurance, life insurance, disability income protection, retirement benefits, sick leave, and paid vacation and holidays.

With a small working staff it may be possible to maintain an informal relationship between employer and employee, but it is best to have a sound working understanding. The employee should know what working rules are, and the employer should have a definite program of employee benefits. If Jim is out for three days with the flu, is he going to be paid, or isn't he? Jim has the right to know what his position is.

What about holidays? Are employees paid for any holidays? And, if so, for how many? What happens in the case of extended illness? surgery? With the cost of medical care and hospitalization caught up in the inflationary spiral, are you, the employer, making any arrangements for your employees to obtain group hospitalization? Some professional photography organizations make a hospitalization plan available to its members.

Disability has always hovered over everyone, as a sort of black cloud that you know is there but you prefer to ignore. There may come a time when disability cannot be ignored. What happens then? Several states have disability insurance programs. There is also a Workman's Compensation program that is paid for by the employer. Both programs are for the benefit of the employee. There usually are, however, time and money limitations to each one. A privately funded disability insurance program will give the employee an income for a guaranteed period of time, which is usually until the disability has ended, or for the remainder of the person's life.

Life insurance policies may be available at preferential rates to some industry groups in your area. While an 18-year-old or 21-year-old person may not be thinking in terms of retirement, it is a very important item to be considered by everyone, employee and employer alike. Many retirement plans are available and they should be carefully investigated. Whether or not employee contributions are required, it can be one of the fringe benefits offered. And the same applies to employee contributions to disability plans, health and hospitalization plans, and life-insurance plans.

Everything that has been mentioned is part of the employment picture. The employer should put himself in the employee's position and then ask himself, "If I were an employee, what would I want?" A happy employee is an asset to an organization. Assets add up to increased income, and after all, that is what business is all about.

The Office Manager

Where is an office manager needed? In every office! Whether you have a one-person business operation or thousands of employees, someone has to take charge of the office.

Let us first consider the one-person operation. That one person is the president, vice-president, secretary, treasurer, supervisor, photographer, darkroom technician, retoucher, shipping clerk, payroll department, accountant, and janitor.

A multiperson business operation takes some of the burden off the single do-it-all and distributes the work load more or less evenly. Now, with specific duties assigned to each person the work flow should be smoother, and the individual burden should be lighter.

What is an office manager? If all the duties are assigned, then what is left to do? An office manager oversees the entire office operation. That includes supervision of the employees and supervision of general business activities. Although the billing clerk is capable of getting the statements into the mail and posting charges and credits, the office manager is the power that wields the hammer on slow or delinquent accounts. The office manager arranges for convenient payments when requested, contacts the firm's attorney or the collection agency for action on delinquents, and keeps tabs on accounts receivable.

The office manager acts as a labor arbitrator and as a listening post for employee problems. Usually a major voice in deciding salary policies goes with the job. The office manager is the central figure in the business operation, taking most of the burden off the shoulders of the photographer-owner. One person may be able to do everything in a small operation, but there are not enough hours in a day for this to carry over into a business that employes several persons.

In some studios, the office manager may also be the receptionist. He or she may schedule all appointments for studio and location photography. The office manager is actually running the entire business with the approval of the boss. It is important to realize that all the inner workings of the business are known to the office manager. It is therefore vital that harmony exist at all times between the owner of the business and the office manager. Losing an office manager to another studio can be compared to the United States losing one of its secret codes.

When does it pay to have an office manager run your office? Only the extent of your operation can determine that, and only you can make the final decision.

Hiring Other Photographers

If you engage photographers for specific assignments, do you hire blindly or do you investigate references? Do you or one of your seasoned employees shoot alongside new photographers for one or two assignments, or do you simply hand them the film and send them out? Do you ask for samples or portfolios?

Some precautions should be taken concerning portfolios. A photographer with a degree from a nationally known school of photography was interviewed. His portfolio was excellent. On his first assignment, as assistant to one of the regular staff members, it was discovered that he did not know how to handle the fast pace of candid shooting demanded by weddings. After several weeks of trial it was decided to let him go. The man couldn't work under the pressures of this type of location shooting. The photographs he did take did not come anywhere near the excellence of his portfolio. Then realization dawned on the studio manager. The student had had a lot of time (in school) in which to prepare the portfolio. That was one of the reasons for its superb quality. But he simply did not fit into a business where different capabilities were needed.

Although photographers are generally tight-lipped when discussing the business aspects of their studios, they do discuss the people whom they engage on a part-time basis. Large corporations investigate the references of job applicants; why shouldn't the studio owner? After all, the photographer is the front line of the studio's financial operation. If you do not have the merchandise, you cannot sell it, no matter how good your proof-passers are and no matter how good your studio facilities are.

The Working Team

What place has gender in your hiring picture? Would you hire a woman as readily as you would a man? Would you hire a man as readily as a woman? Although most male photographers will tell you they have not experienced any, or many, problems while working in the bridal rooms, there are times when women clients relate better to women but others when men relate better to women. I believe a lot of the pre-wedding nervous reactions of the bridegroom and his party can be solved with a woman photographer. Whereas the male group may bark at a male photographer attempting to obtain some of the posed pre-ceremony shots, they might be more cooperative with a female photographer. Therefore, a good working team could be "one of each." Realistically, gender should not enter into the hiring situation at all. The photographer that is hired should be the best one.

Another aspect of photography where availability of photographers of both sexes is a definite asset is in legal-medical malpractice work. Otherwise it is advisable to have a woman assistant present when a woman is to be photographed by a male photographer, and vice versa. In hospitals, nurses and orderlies can be pressed into service. But how about the ninety-five percent of the time when this photography is done outside the hospital? Again, the one-of-each team would seem ideal.

Protection photography, where the contents of homes are photographed, is another place where a woman photographer is a definite asset. The homemaker is usually present while the contents are being photographed, and she might be glad to have another woman in the working team.

What Assistants Can Do

While most wedding photographers shoot on location without assistants, those who do use them extol the virtue of having a "gofor"—that is, a person who *goes for* this, *goes for* that, *goes for* anything the photographer may need while shooting. The assistant can also help the photographer be in two places at once, such as when the bride's father hands her over to the bridegroom. Sometimes both parents will kiss the bride, then she will take her new escort's arm and proceed to the altar. That exchange is the place for two or three shots, and two shots taken from two views are often more effective than two shots taken from a single camera position.

If photography is permitted during the ceremony, it is advantageous to have one photographer at the altar taking the ring and vow shots while the other can be down the aisle taking the very effective, and beautiful, long shots. If both photographers are at the same location, then one can have the camera set for strobe (if allowed) while the other is geared for natural light. Using two photographers and two cameras for this operation not only takes a lot of strain off the single photographer in readjusting shutter speeds and *f*-stops; it also minimizes the likelihood of error.

Later, at the reception, tossing of the bouquet and the garter are other places where two photographers work to the advantage of added sales: One photographer catches the toss from the rear, including eager spectators' faces, while the other snaps it from the front. You have two photographs for each part of the action, the toss and the catch.

Setting up table shots is much easier with the aid of an assistant. This is also true with groups that are to be photographed. Any wedding, at best, is a hurried affair in that it is a one-shot deal, with no retakes. An assistant can do much to lighten the burden of the principal photographer and also be there with additional equipment in case of emergency. It may cost a little more to add an assistant to the assignment, but the added advantages and increased sales will reimburse you. In the long run it is not really a luxury.

CHAPTER 13 Communications

One of the important factors in human relationships is communication. Marriages have failed, social relationships have sustained hiatuses, and international diplomatic relations have been strained by a lack of, or a break in, communication.

How is your business line of communication? Do you have an open line at all times? Can you be reached when you are not in the office or studio? Is your phone always "covered" for incoming calls? While portrait and commercial photography can be regulated during a specified working schedule, legal photography cannot be time-controlled. The need for a photographer to record an accident can arise at any time.

People often "communicate" only in a one-way direction—pointed their way. A harried studio owner once called for help. He had overextended himself by contracting several jobs over a wide geographical area. Within 15 minutes, the person to whom he had turned for help had covered every assignment with photographers. Many of the calls were out of the area, at toll charges, but they were made without hesitation or any request for reimbursement. Yet the harried studio owner did not have the decency, or the courtesy, to pick up the phone and thank his benefactor. No call to say a simple, "Thank you." Communication was present when help was needed. Why wasn't it there afterward?

One particular studio that specializes in commercial photography will not do wedding photography even for close friends. "It just isn't our cup of tea," the owner remarked. "We recommend other local photographers for the work." He then commented that, besides never sending a note of thanks for the potential business, many of the local photographers never bothered calling the leads that were furnished.

Every bit of important information should be noted on a pad, a large calendar, or somewhere. One successful businessman insists that all phone messages are to be noted and the important points excerpted and filed in the client's folder. The notes can be reviewed and used as required. (Review the start of Chapter 12 for more telephone tips.)

First Acquaintance

How is your telephone answered? Is the caller greeted pleasantly—"Good morning, XYZ Studio, our lines are busy. Can you hold a moment, please?" Or, is the caller stunned by a rapid-fire barrage of words such as, "XYZ Studio hold," followed by a clicking noise and then silence? Not only does the caller have absolutely no chance to speak one word, but also he or she may remain in that wordless vacuum for an indefinite period of time. Perhaps the call is long distance, or an emergency. No telephone call should be put on "hold" until the person has had a chance to state the reason for the call.

Many is the time that a call has been held and forgotten. One receptionist went on a coffee break while a caller floated in a world of silence. The prospective client tired of the silent treatment called another studio. Studio number two, practicing correct business manners, gained a customer.

Another side of the telephone scene takes place in the studio. Does the receptionist continue talking on the telephone while customers are waiting in the reception room for assistance or information? Are personal telephone calls interfering with business calls?

Staying in Touch

If several months have elapsed since your previous assignment from a normally active client, do you pass it off or do you follow through? Follow-through can be accomplished in several ways. You can telephone "just to say hello"; you can send an informal greeting card; or, if you are in the neighborhood, you can stop in, spend a few minutes in conversation, and renew your contact.

Another way is the business lunch. There is absolutely nothing wrong with it, it may promote business, and it is tax-deductible.

Communication in any form is the backbone of doing business in today's business world.

CHAPTER 14

Customer Relations

It has often been asked why one person can be a top-notch salesperson with ninety-eight percent of the customers and fail with two percent? On the other hand, someone else who fails with ninety-eight percent may sell the two percent that the first person "lost." Why can a person with inferior merchandise sometimes walk away with a contract?

Much of it has something to do with what is often called "vibrations." A salesperson's voice, manner of dress, grooming, attitude, and other such points are, in large measure, responsible for the success or failure of many deals. Voice can often be the deciding factor, especially in telephone contacts.

How to Close a Sale

How can you tell if you have landed the job? When should you try to close the sale? The first item to be considered is the rapport between you and the prospective customer. Assuming that the need for photography is not immediate, which could force the customer to take the first deal that either appealed or met certain criteria, what creates rapport?

Many things enter the sales picture. While the young, inexperienced, and sometimes brash, salesperson may close a few good sales, most such successes can be attributed to luck. The experienced salesperson knows when a customer is price-shopping, when a person is sincere, when to deliver the closing pitch, and when to hand the contract and a pen to the customer. A good salesperson also knows when to pack everything up and walk out.

About those vibrations: One client may remark, "I get good vibes when I talk to Joan." Mrs. Smith asks that Frank handle her photography arrangements: "I like Frank. We understand each other." What these people are trying to say is that there is a person-to-person balance that makes for a good working relationship. Whether or not you believe in extra-sensory perception (E.S.P.) or any other psychic phenomena—and it is not the intent of the author to influence the reader in any direction—it remains a fact that two persons meeting for the first time can, without speaking a single word, reach the same conclusion that they can get along with each other. That is why salespersons are often switched on a prospective customer. Where one couldn't close the deal, the other could.

In your own business, if a customer irritates you, or if you see that you irritate the customer, it is best to let someone else handle the negotiations. What starts out as a reception-room barrier could become an on-the-job obstruction.

Let us assume you and the customer are getting along well. You are presenting the information asked for. After you have explained the various services your company will perform, hand the customer a copy of your contract. Now he or she has one of two alternatives: sign the contract, or leave. This is not pushing the sale. At this point the sale has been either made or lost. What you are doing is bringing the issue to a head. You are going for the close. Your time is worth money, so why tie it up with non-revenue-producing talk? Believe it or not, with experience you can actually feel the right moment to go for the close.

Selectivity is a two-way street. Just as the customer has the privilege of selecting the person who is going to provide the wanted services, so, too, does the merchant or vendor of these services have privileges. There are successful wedding photographers who actually choose which clients they will accept.

The Shop-at-Home Ploy

There is a practice in many localities of shopping at home. A person planning a wedding or a social event telephones to several vendors and asks them to call in person. The vendors go to the home laden with samples, present their sales talk, and hope their efforts will be rewarded with a signed contract.

Well, it usually doesn't work out that way. Instead of going from one shop to another, which is time consuming, the prospective customers remain in the comfort of home. Within the safety of their own surroundings they have no hesitation about telling a vendor "they would like to think about it." This closes the chapter on that sale. In the store, the salesperson has the advantage of having the customer in "strange" surroundings. The potential client must walk out of the store to break off negotiations. This is a decided advantage for the salesperson.

One photographer tired of home appointments during the evening, on Sundays or holidays, rain or shine. After several months he called a halt. His receptionist stated the hours when the studio was open and suggested an appointment. His business actually increased.

Another habit that needs bringing under control is telephone quotations. How can anyone make a decision on different photographers without seeing their work? The reply to a price request might be: "Sorry, but we do not quote prices over the phone. Would you like to make an appointment so that we can show you our fine photography?" Believe it or not, a caller's "no" to that question would not mean that you could have had the job if you had given the information. Although most of today's comparison shopping is done by telephone, the serious buyer is the one who wants to see the merchandise before talking money. Remember what was said before: Selectivity is a two-way street.

Education

CHAPTER 15

A good basic education is the foundation and the beginning of one's career. Many people think that the diploma or degree is the end of the educational process. They lose sight of the fact that education continues through our entire lifetime. Indeed, for every day that we can say we have learned one new thing, we have accomplished something.

On the other hand, it is a good idea to continue formal education. This is possible through graduate studies; through seminars presented by professionals who offer practical, on-the-job, experience; or through the many schools that offer "extension courses." These may, or may not, be taught on campus. They may, or may not, earn credits for a degree. The important fact is that they are being offered.

Many of today's photographers started out in other fields—engineering, teaching, real estate, sales, banking, medicine, plumbing, truck driving, and so on ad infinitum. Until recently, very few attended schools where photography was a major course of study. In most schools of higher education, photography is still thought of as an adjunct, and the degree is conferred in Fine Arts, Journalism or Communications. Among the exceptions are the Brooks Institute of Photographic Art and Science in Santa Barbara, California, and the Rochester (New York) Institute of Technology. Both offer degrees in photography.

The basic foundation. Education is needed in the fundamentals of the science and of the art of photography. If photography is an art form, then the photographer should be well versed in proportions and shapes, values of light, composition, posing, and many of the other aspects of art that are also necessary to paintings or sketches. The basic science courses are chemistry, physics, mathematics, and geometry, to name a few. The photojournalist goes one step further, adding courses in writing.

As can be seen, photography is no longer a stepchild. A basic formal education should be obtained before the person seeking a career in this discipline goes on to the practical part. Although this has not been the case in the past, it is now becoming a reality. Last accepted practice for someone desiring to become a professional photographer was to pick up a camera and start shooting. By trial and error, by perseverance, by sheer guts, the person mastered the art of photography.

Apprenticeships. Another method, popular in Europe, was apprenticeship. As an example, let us take the case of Emil. He was apprenticed to a photographer at the age of nine. Emil swept floors, cleaned chemical trays, stocked supplies, and was the general handyman. When he was eleven he was allowed to make his first proofs. At fifteen, Emil snapped the shutter of the studio view camera for the first time.

Emil was taught lighting, composition, oil painting, sketching, restorations, mathematics, chemistry, and a multitude of other subjects. This was his entire formal education. He never attended any academic institution. Emil was a photographer in the United States for several decades. He was a true craftsman. He was an artisan. When he died, his craft died with him because no such lengthy apprenticeship program exists in this country.

Let us return to the basics of the darkroom. A professional photographer must know how to make a photographic print. The photographer should know what it takes to produce what is really wanted. Then, after mastering the mechanics of the darkroom, the photographer can devote time to perfecting technique behind the camera. The photographer and the darkroom technician must be able to work together as a team.

Learning never stops. What about those who are now practicing photography without benefit of the educational processes described above? They should attend seminars and learn from others. But herein lies another danger: imitation. We must learn, and go on to improve, and develop our own individuality in our work.

Many excellent courses in photography are now being offered across the country. There are short ones and long ones, there are one-day seminars and week-long class sessions and summer schools. The Professional Photographers of America school at Winona, Indiana, and the West Coast School of the Professional Photographers of California are only two of the places where a photographer of any level of competence can further his education: There are more every year.

Doctors, dentists, lawyers, and engineers, to name a few other professionals, do not sit upon past laurels. They attend seminars from time to time in order to upgrade their knowledge. They go to learn of the latest advances in their fields. Our world is moving so rapidly that the information we received yesterday is probably obsolete today. If you wouldn't read last week's newspapers to know what is going on around you today, then how can you be content with the education you received five or ten years ago? Education is enlightenment, and continuing education is a must if we are to keep up and to progress. You can either keep swimming or get swept aside by the waves generated by those who pass you by.

CHAPTER 16 Equipment

What does your equipment inventory look like? Are you still working with one of those tried-and-true Brownie box cameras, or are you working with Nikons, Hasselblads, Pentaxes, Canons, Linhofs, Calumets, and the rest? Are you developing film in a dingy back closet, or are you using one of the modern, efficient, professional laboratories? Or have you a well-equipped lab as part of your business operation? Do you hold old equipment together with baling wire, solder, and a prayer, or do you constantly trade your used equipment in for updated models?

Another question to ask yourself is: Why do amateurs seem to have better cameras, lenses, and strobes than professionals do? A possible answer suggested by a salesman at a photography convention was that the working professional had to justify equipment purchases by projected use for production of income. The amateur did not have to consider this factor. If the amateur wanted to modernize (or upgrade) his equipment, and had the money to do so, those two factors were the only considerations.

That analysis is basically correct—and that is the sad part of it. The number of rolls of film that a professional puts through one of his cameras in one month is probably greater than the number the amateur puts through all of his cameras in one *year.* Another variable is the amount of use each person gives his equipment. Some amateur-owned equipment never sees the service shop, while the professional counterpart may be there every six months or oftener.

Amateur vs. Professional. It is no wonder that, with today's advanced technology, the amateur can sometimes run circles around the professional. The expertise to create the photograph may be within the individual, but equipment *is* needed to do the job. We are not considering the prestige value of appearing on location with the latest equipment. We are not considering the prestige value of having the latest equipment in our studio. We are considering the advantages the latest equipment offers in the way of working tools that will make our work easier and better. That should be the first thought when we review our equipment. A job is easy if you have the know-how and the right tools; but no matter how much know-how a master craftsman may have, the simplest job can turn out to be a tough one without proper equipment.

Help from I.R.S. Another factor to consider is the tax advantage gained in updating equipment. If your accountant is depreciating your equipment over a five-year period, it would be advantageous to sell your old models and purchase new equipment after the depreciation period. If you don't, you will be paying out that portion of your income in some form of tax.

Care and planning. Equipment reliability begins with a sensible maintenance program. Waiting until equipment breaks down on the job is definitely not a sensible maintenance program. You will want to plan a service schedule for your cameras according to the amount of use, type of environment, and method of handling the equipment. A news photographer with eight Nikons can have two in the shop at all times. Then there is at least one wedding photographer who operates with a single Rollei that he carries in a canvas bag in the trunk of his car. The camera has never seen the inside of a service shop in the 15 years since he purchased it. You do hear of such cases. But most professional photographers work with more than a single camera.

Regular maintenance of equipment is required for dependability in emergencies. Don't let the camera that looks as though it was run over by a Sherman tank fool you. The newspaper photographer who owns it has it checked at regular intervals. To him that piece of equipment is his bread and butter.

Carrying double. Another type of insurance against equipment failure is to carry duplicate equipment. Sync and strobe power cords are famous for failing in emergency situations. If a cord fails tie it in a knot and toss it into the first trash basket you find. Don't give any thought to repairing it: A lost shot that cannot be redone is not worth an unreliable cord, regardless of replacement cost.

The same is true for batteries. We seem to be more dependent upon batteries of all sizes and shapes with each passing day. With all our sophisticated equipment, what happens when the batteries fail? Total blackout! Our automatic cameras stop, the exposure meters stop, and *we* stop, unless we have some assistance. That assistance comes in the form of our education, training, expertise, and manual override on as much of the automatic equipment as possible. And a good bit of insurance is to carry a non-battery-operated exposure meter in your equipment case.

To be sure is to be safe. To be safe is a very comfortable feeling. It is better to be safe than to be sorry.

Your Processing Lab

CHAPTER 17

Many years ago a photographer commented that successful studio operation was a marriage of the photographer and the darkroom assistant. The idea was that the photographer could make more money with the camera while on location, or in the posing room of the studio, than when tied down in the darkroom.

There were, naturally, some conditions. The photographer should be proficient in darkroom procedures, including film handling, processing, chemicals, printing, and how to achieve special effects. The photographer had to know what could be accomplished in the darkroom—and what should be done in the viewfinder of the camera. The photographer and the darkroom assistant together needed an efficient system of communication and a good working relationship.

Who should process? Many photographers scoff at the idea of anyone other than themselves touching their negatives or transparencies. They tell stories of "acetate torture," damage, and lost film. They may have good reason to be concerned for the safety of their materials; but how many photographers can honestly state that they themselves have *never* damaged film during handling or processing? The pros and cons of using commercial processing labs can be tossed around until we all retire from active participation in this business. The truth is that the busy photographer does not have time to take the photograph and then turn out all the end products all alone. Each of us must find and follow the path that is best for our individual purposes.

When all the work was black and white, the photographer would crop the proof and produce a representative sample of the finished photograph. This took a lot of time, but living conditions seemed less hurried in those computerless days. A two-stop transcontinental flight was considered luxury as measured against a train trip of several days. Today, some persons think five hours are too much for that same flight, even with nonstop service.

Along came color. When color photography started to become established, many photographers decided to convert their black-and-white darkrooms to color. This involved a large capital investment and, usually, the hiring of additional workers. A lab, in order to pay its own way, must be operating most of the time, as the small studio owner who installed a color lab soon found out. In order to support the lab, processing was solicitated from other studios. Often this, worked against the total setup because competitors for the photographic dollar were now engaged in business together and against each other at the same time. Labs failed and relationships—never too cordial to begin with—were ruptured completely.

There were cases where combination processor-studios became pirates, underbidding jobs that other studios were bidding on. The lab profit margin shrank as bids were lowered.

From this apparent chaos evolved the professional processing lab as we know it today. These laboratories are full-service operations with a complement of specialists that few photographers could afford to employ, even on a part-time basis.

Let us look at some of the services top-notch labs offer their customers. The retouching, or art, department is a vital link in the photographic process. If you have ever had a blinker, then you know how frustrating the situation can be. Through the art of retouching, eyes can appear where only eyelids were before. We are also offered print mounting, texturing, spraying—all the special treatments so popular with the buying public. Mutiple-unit printing, made possible by cluster lenses, is another feature offered by many labs. Can any but the largest studios afford to purchase the equipment necessary for these operations, and also hire the qualified personnel to perform the duties and services? The answer is obvious.

Working with a lab. When you first begin working with a laboratory, don't expect miracles. There is going to be a *getting acquainted* period. They have to get to know you: how you shoot, what you need in the finished product. On the other hand, you must know exactly what they can and what they cannot do. They are not photographers, and to expect them to rectify your camera errors to make you appear a master photographer is asking too much.

A good photographer should know what is involved in processing photographic materials. He should ask himself if he could go into the darkroom and come out with the end product he wants. Knowledge of the "manufacture" of the photographic print or the transparency is vital to the successful photographer. Only by knowing what is involved can he effectively communicate with lab personnel.

Certain operations use black and white almost entirely. News, public relations, and photography done at conventions are some of the best-known applications. Convention photography is still almost all done in black and white, although some color is beginning to be used. One reason is speed: Newspapers need photographs "right now," and black-and-white work fills that requirement. Another is cost: Color may be added for special additions to the regular newspaper, such as the Sunday magazine section, or for the flyers paid for by advertisers.

There is a definite need for doing your own lab work, and also a definite need for the commercial or custom processing laboratories. Your own business will determine how you schedule your work flow. Everything must work to your advantage or it is of no advantage to you.

CHAPTER 18 Pricing

One of the keys to solvency—keeping the business operating in black ink rather than red ink—is pricing. "Here," "astuteness" is the key word. Facts and figures, which may sound dull in accounting, are the lifeline of your business when you have to consider your pricing schedule.

Many people have a curious way of obtaining their first pricing schedule when they start out in business: They make countless telephone calls to other photographers, pretending they are prospective customers, or visit studios with their daughters, or their girl or boy friends, saying they plan a wedding in the "not too distant future." The experienced business person can usually spot the information seekers almost immediately, in the way they ask questions and the way they act in the studio. Some are constantly making notations, others request as many price lists as possible to take with them.

A few professional associations do have pricing guides for their members. It has been found, however, that the figures in the guides are so far off they could not be used even as a base from which to start. If the going rate for commercial photography in your area is \$75 per hour, then how can you honestly expect to charge the \$100 to \$150 per hour shown in the guide? A few established photographers do command \$1000 to \$1500 or more dollars per day for their time, but they are in the minority. You cannot expect a client to pay \$25 for a color print when other photographers in your area are asking \$15. Therefore, the question is: Where do I begin to work out an intelligent price schedule? That word "intelligent" is where you begin.

If a print cost me \$5 as it came from the lab, could I give it to you "at cost" for \$5?

Analyze Costs

Let us reconsider the cost of this print. The \$5 is the price for the raw print. What about spotting fees, shipping charges, and the cost of carrying the transaction through your books? Have you considered the cost of the check with which you pay the lab, postage, the return envelope, and bookkeeping?

How about handling? Someone had to mark the proof for cropping, burning, or other treatment.

Someone had to put the negative into a lab envelope, which had to be properly marked. The lab envelope had to be sent or delivered to the processing lab. That all took time. Then, when the order was returned, someone had to open the package, check the contents, enter the statement in the bookeeping system, and do something with the negative—if the studio's, replace it in the file; if the customer's, return it with the print. Assuming a folder is needed for the print, there are the cost of the folder and the costs involved in obtaining and storing it. And so on. Who pays these labor and miscellaneous costs? If you have hired help, you are paying them for the time they spend at work. If you do not, *you* will be doing the work, and who is going to pay you?

Here are some additional factors to consider: rent, utilities, insurance, equipment—both cost and maintenance. To remain in business, you have to include these expenses when computing prices.

Now you have an entirely different picture of what an item really costs. The lab fee may be $5, but the actual cost, without any profit margin, may be $7 or $10, more or less. The important thing to keep in mind is that the cost of the print is not what you pay the lab.

Overhead expenses have to be computed in order to be able to add an intelligent percentage onto every item leaving your place of business and every service performed by you or one of your employees. There are many ways to arrive at this figure. Let's take one method as an example.

Let us assume the following expenses:

Rent:	$ 750.00 per month
Telephone:	$ 100.00 per month average
Electric:	$ 100.00 per month average
Water:	$ 35.00 per month average
Gas (heat):	$ 35.00 per month average
TOTAL:	$1020.00 per month average expenses

Let us also assume that we have a receptionist with a salary of $200 per 40-hour week. Add medical plan insurance, Workman's Compensation, and taxes, and the cost will be around $250. Let's convert from monthly to weekly figuring by dividing our $1020 montly average by 4⅓ weeks per month. The resultant figure is $235.38, which we can round off. Adding the receptionist's adjusted salary of $250 to $235, we now have $485 average weekly expenses.

Assuming that we do three weddings or other such events per week, at an average tab of $750 each, plus other in-house work of $500, we now have a total weekly income of $2750. If we divide $485 by $2750 we arrive at the percentage figure of 17.64, or 18%. This means you must take 18% of your gross sales to cover your expenses. And that does not include film or equipment, maintenance, your salary, professional association dues, or profit margin.

Taking the raw print out of the lab at $5, let us add 20% plus $2.50 for shipping and handling charges ($1.50 by the lab and approximately $1 at your end). We now have $8.50 for the print, to which we must add the price of the folder, if that item was requested. If the folder wholesales at $.50, and we add 20% for a total of $.60, the actual wholesale price of the $5 print is now $9.10. The reason for using 20% instead of 18% here is to cover bank activity charges and postage. If you have a bookkeeper or an accountant, their fees must be included, too.

Where Is the Profit?

Remember that in all we have done thus far you have not received one cent for profit or for your salary, yet the price of the print has almost doubled. If you released the product for your lab fee only, you would be paying for doing someone a favor. While it is acceptable to do favors for friends and relatives, you certainly could not stay in operation very long using such business practices. Therefore, if a friend asks you to do a favor and make a print, add the operating percentage to the price of the raw print and state *that* figure as your *actual cost* price. They won't believe you are not making a handsome profit; so, with that attitude, you have one other alternative: Make a profit. Add another 20% to the price. Carrying on with the same example, this would mean billing $10.92—or $11, rounded off.

Many articles have been written about price factors. Perhaps you already know about them. In essence, price factors are multipliers used to compute selling prices from the cost of material. For instance, if the materials for photographing a wedding cost you $125, then your price should be $375, $500, $625, or more, depending upon which factor you used—3, 4, or 5. You can arrive at your own factor by taking into consideration all of your expenses, plus your profit margin, plus your salary. If that figure, in percent, brings a $150-material-cost job to $450, then your factor is 3. Going back to our earlier example, the factor applied was 2.2 (5 basic cost × 2.2 = $11).

The use of factors is supposed to be a "fast math" system for calculating prices. It does not work in all instances, however. For example, what factor do you use where photographic services are itemized separately from material costs? Or when, in legal photography, the photographer is called into court to testify, or is asked to give a deposition concerning the person photographed? The photographer who spends time in court or in making depositions must be compensated, the same as a lawyer or a doctor is compensated for the time spent with the same legal matters. How do you think their fees are computed? When asked about this, one doctor remarked, "I am selling so many minutes of time, and my time is worth X amount per minute." Well, the photographer must also learn to "sell minutes of time."

The Bottom Line

There is really nothing mysterious about pricing. It is a simple matter of sitting down and figuring what the item actually costs you to put out. Once you have worked out the percentage or factor, your price schedules can be easily established.

CHAPTER 19

The Profit Picture

One of the keys to profits is the way in which a photographer does an assignment. He has to know what shots are important, what will generally sell, and what will sell particularly well. If the hosts say, "No table shots," then that is the final word. One photographer was told the client did not like dance-floor shots because they had "too many backs." The photographer took the hint and made certain the principals were facing the camera when he snapped the shutter. In fact, the shots were posed; but the finished results looked natural. The photographer had picked the right type of dance and the right moment, and all the dance photos were accepted by the customer.

An overabundance of exposures can deplete profits. It was true in 1975, when this author described it in an article in *Studio Photography* magazine ("Shooting Holes in the Profit Net," *September 1975*), and it is true today. Every job is estimated by the number of photographs the client desires. You certainly would not make only 24 exposures for an estimated order of 24 eight-by-ten prints; but neither would you shoot 240 frames for the same 24-photograph order. Although my philosophy has always been that film is the cheapest photographic commodity, everything depends upon the total number of photographs specified in the purchase order: When the client says, "No table shots," then you most definitely do not waste film and time on the groups at the tables.

There is usually no reason for a photographer to take more than two shots of any group of ten or fewer persons. The exception is if there is equipment trouble or if the photographer notices some definite fault in the grouping. If you have large groups—25 or more—then six exposures should be the maximum. No matter how many shots you take the results will always be the same: Someone will blink, someone will be looking anywhere except at the photographer, someone will be standing on the edges of his feet, someone will slip a hand around the next person's waist, etc. And even if these "mishaps" do not occur you will still wind up with a lot of duplicates that will have to be culled.

During the wedding processional the photographer usually has one shot at any of the principals, and (surprisingly) 99% of those exposures are good. Then why should there be more than two shots of a group of four persons?

How to Avoid Conflict

Another cause of revenue loss on location is the snapshooter. The professional photographer sets up the scene, then either before, during, or after the pro's session a snapshooter may creep forward and fire off his or her camera at the scene composed by the professional. Too often a client will use those amateur photos to send to relatives because they can get duplicates for much less than they would have to pay the studio for prints. This is a delicate situation, and the manner in which it is handled by the photographer is important. Although your contract contains a clause prohibiting any other photographers from taking photographs while the professional photographer is on the job, the guests are probably not aware of this. One way to inform them is by distributing printed cards specifically stating that the host has a contract with the photographer and requesting that camera gear be stowed. (A sample card is shown in Chapter 3, in connection with Item 12 and Item 16 of the standard contract.)

Well, what happens if you have followed these steps and the errant person still refuses to put the camera away? One enterprising photographer found a solution when confronted with a physician who was table hopping. The doctor wanted to send photos to the folks back home. He also wanted to send photos of the new couple, of the bride in the bridal room, of some of the assembled guests, and of the dancing. The host talked to his guest, but to no avail. Then the photographer had an idea. He approached the physician, and the following conversation took place:

"You could probably spin circles around me as a photographer, Doctor Smith; however, I have a job to do and a living to earn. I would appreciate your stowing the camera gear until after I have completed my assignment."

"You can't make me put my camera away."

"Well, we do have a contract with the hosts."

"You know what you can do with that piece of paper."

"Doc," the photographer said then, "you go ahead and take all the photographs you want today. Monday morning when you get to your office you'll find me in the hallway with a bridge table set up. I'll have a selection of over-the-counter drug preparations and a sign that says, 'I am a photographer playing doctor.' "

The doctor looked at the photographer, and extended his hand in apology.

"You've made your point very succinctly. I did not realize I was cutting into your income. I apologize." He walked over to his equipment bag and put the camera and strobe away.

The successful photographer must know something about human psychology. We are working with people, and no two are alike. We must apply ourselves to each situation and to each individual, and we must do it in such a manner as to win over the other person. We use psychology to make our jobs easier, and the result also tends to increase the take for the cash register.

Sales and Marketing

CHAPTER 20

This chapter has several sections because the entire concept is too large to be treated in one package.

When people think about the word "sales" they often think in terms of a special-price event at a department store or bargains at a local merchant's shop. They think of newspaper ads and flyers. We have been conditioned by the advertising industry to make this association.

The general term *"sales"* encompasses everything that has to do with the offering of products and services by a business enterprise. Whatever is sold is part of the sales picture. In order for a business to prosper, the sales picture must be a bright one.

It should be kept in mind that sales depend, to a large extent, upon marketing and merchandising, and that merchandising includes many different forms of customer enticement.

Merchandising enters the scene because without effective merchandising you have neither a bright sales picture nor a good future. Turn that around: With effective merchandising you have a bright sales picture and a good future. Let's examine what's involved.

Direct Advertising

Sales promotion is the basis of merchandising. For example: You have beautiful business cards printed. What good do they do in your pocket? Those business cards are part of the overall advertising scheme, but in order to do any good they must be distributed. It is the same with printed flyers. If 1000 are left on someone's desk, they are worthless. But if you were to walk through a supermarket parking lot, placing one flyer on each automobile, then they could become effective. Even a 1% return makes an effort worthwhile; and the greater the exposure, the greater the potential return.

How do you advertise? Word-of-mouth advertising by satisfied clients is good, but it will not keep you in business very long. The exposure is not great enough. An established studio in a business district can use its windows for advertising, as they are exposed to a great many passing shoppers. This is still not enough, however. What about the studio-in-a-home operation? Here you do not even have the "walk-in trade" but have to rely upon recommendations and other sorts of advertising.

First on the list of advertising media is the classified telephone directory—the Yellow Pages. A large segment of the buying public shops through the Yellow Pages. Directories are usually changed every year; so you should plan your ad carefully. It must be attractive and distinctive. It must draw prospective customers to your telephone number.

Promoting Party Assignments

How does the wedding photographer get his name known? Many of those starting in business tie in with a caterer, a catering establishment, or a party coordinator who arranges a variety of events, not just weddings.

Coordinators frequently operate as manager of the event, supplying all necessary products and services. Sometimes there is a professional fee arrangement in effect: The coordinator acts as sales representative and so is entitled to a comission on any sales resulting to the photographer from the event. Some photographers may be associated with more than one coordinator.

Associating with caterers is another way of establishing a business. Here, as with the party coordinator, certain rules may operate. A catering establishment usually receives a commission. Some offer package deals, in which all the necessary space, services, and products are provided under one agreement, and the caterer contracts for the musicians, the florist, the photographer, etc. Many states do not permit such package deals. With consumer advocates now on the lookout to protect customers, it may be that all states will adopt legislation against the all-inclusive party package.

Many photographers who started out in association with party coordinators or catering establishments continue working this way. For some this may be a main source of income, while for others it may be the gravy. A good coordinator or catering place can keep a photographer busy every weekend of the year. One Los Angeles coordinator, for instance, runs some eight to twelve parties on most weekends. And a large catering establishment, with six banquet rooms, has its calendar full for a year in advance. Translated into photography jobs, those figures suddenly become very large.

The Portrait Market

Portrait photographers who have store-studios don't usually favor door-to-door sales. One enterprising photographer, however, an ex-coupon-passer himself, decided to open his own studio on the basis of this premise: People will generally not pass up what they think is a bargain. Effective public relations established, in the minds of the area's upper-middle-income residents, the fact that this photographer was something out of the ordinary. The word was that his portraits were desirable, that every home had to have one or more hanging on the walls. His prices were established on a high plane: $45 for an 8″ x 10″ print plus $25 for the sitting fee. The time was the first half of the 1970s, when $70 for a single 8″ × 10″ color photograph was not exactly a bargain price. How did he achieve this?

The sample prints in the studio were 16″ × 20″ and larger in size. In fact, 30″ × 40″ was not uncommon. Then, his receptionist could have been a graduate of some "Madison Avenue School of Advertising," as she knew every trick in the book on how to make a customer part with the last cent in pocket or purse. Together, they made a highly successful team.

So where did this photographer differ from any other ambitious photographer with a good studio location, a nice display of photographs, and an astute businesswoman-receptionist? He had a gimmick. The gimmick was coupons.

Several times a year a coupon passer would visit the surrounding residential areas, selling an 8″ × 10″ color portrait for $10. The sales campaign was arranged so that the coupon passer did not visit any area more than once in any 12-month period. The salesperson sold the coupon and kept the entire $10 as the sales commission. One half of the sales receipt was given to the purchaser and the other half was returned to the studio.

Here is where the full sales technique came into play. The coupon purchaser, having put down the $10, had to make an appointment for the sitting. When the person called for the appointment, he or she was informed that the entire family would be photographed at the same time—at no additional cost. Arguments such as, "But all I want is a single picture," were no use. The reply was something like, "We are not going to charge you for the other shots, we just like to photograph entire families together." A coupon holder who stuck to insisting upon a photograph for a single family member would be informed that, because of camera setups at the present time, the family group could be done in about three weeks, whereas a single-portrait appointment was three or four months distant. So what happened?

The appointment was made and the entire family showed up at the appointed time. The customer was cautioned to arrive at least half an hour early. If the appointment were missed there would probably be a two or three month wait because of the studio's heavy schedule.

At this studio persons arriving for their portrait appointment do not share the same reception area as those who are examining their proofs. No proofs leave the building. There are no exceptions to this rule. People who are at the studio for the first time, and clients examining proofs, are both treated to something out of the books on merchandising: Final orders are carried out of the studio in full view of everyone else—for good reason: Most of the orders are framed in sizes 24″ × 30″ or 30″ × 40″ and accompanied by an assortment of 11″ × 14″, 8″ × 10″, and miscellaneous wallet-sized prints. Very impressive—and tempting.

When the whole family is photographed, the usual procedure is to take individual shots of each child, of each parent, of both parents, of all the children as a group, and then of the entire family. If you were to ask why the double talk about not being able to make an appointment for a single person's photograph, and yet here singles were being taken, you would not get a reply that made sense: It was another gimmick: to get a whole family into the studio. And then—how many parents would pick a single 8″ × 10″

of one child and none of the other? Remember, only one coupon was sold per family. Very few customers end up with the single 8″ × 10″ photograph offered by the coupon. Most of the outgoing orders conclude in the range between $300 and $750.

Another merchandising gimmick is frames. All 8″ × 10″ and larger photographs are mounted in frames when the customer calls for the order. If the customer accepts the frame, or another that is in stock, a "fantastic" 10% discount is allowed on the frame–which has been marked up to double the wholesale price. If the customer decides to forego the frames and perhaps go home to talk it over with the spouse, then the discount offer is off. This is true high-pressure sales-pitching in high gear. There is nothing illegal about the operation, and the only thing that will put such an operator out of business is an end to the public's greed for a bargain.

Other Publicity Media

Another type of sales-promotion activity is direct-mail advertising. In this operation you depend upon mailing lists to get your sales brochure into the hands of prospective customers. Bulk-mailing rates are relatively inexpensive, provided you can take the time to presort it by ZIP code. The greatest expenditure may be the mailing lists. Either you can purchase the lists outright, or a firm specializing in bulk mailings will do the entire job for you and all you supply is your advertising literature.

The immediate effect of bulk mailing is that a wide area can be served, the number of persons covered in one mailing far exceeding the number that can be contacted by the door-to-door approach. There is one decided advantage to the direct personal approach, however: The salesperson uses his or her ability to actually sell you, the photographer, to the public.

High schools are a good source of future engagement and wedding business. They are also good sources of income for the portrait photographer in another way: Many seniors who do not like their "official" senior portraits will patronize a studio of their own choice.

Churches, synagogues, and large meeting halls are other places that should be investigated. If a church is known for an abundance of weddings, then leave some of your business cards, some flyers, and, where appropriate, a few framed samples of your work.

Bridal shops, gift shops, places that sell silverware and crystal, are other good leads. Just remember that you want to place your literature where it will do you the most good, and that place is not in your studio.

If you specialize in pictures of babies or children, try placing your literature in stores that sell maternity clothes, baby clothes, baby shoes, etc. Try offering a coupon to new mothers. First you photograph the newborn infant, then you work on the "interval program," where a child is photographed at specific age intervals or at stated times during the year. This gives the family a growth record. Many baby-photography plans follow this procedure.

For ideas on where to place your advertising, begin with the letter "A" in the Yellow Pages of your telephone directory. You would be surprised at the amount of information available in that handy volume. Nowadays it certainly isn't beneath professional dignity to try the supermarket-parking-lot distribution method mentioned before for flyers. There are local newspapers and specialty magazines, too.

The kind and amount of advertising you do will depend upon what you have available to spend on it. When you hear the slogan "It pays to advertise," you'd better believe it.

Commercial and Specialty Photographers.

The commercial photographer does not usually follow the same lines of advertising and sales promotion as the portrait photographer. The entire scope of operations is different from that involving portraits, weddings, and general social-event photography. The commercial photographer works with advertising agencies, manufacturers, designers, and other business clients.

For discussion purposes, commercial photography includes fashion, food, and illustrative photography. In lieu of flyers, a person wanting to become established as a commercial photographer will usually have a portfolio and will visit prospective clients in person. If the photographer can tie in with an advertising agency, the agency may give him jobs for a number of its clients. Having several agencies as customers can keep a good photographer busy. As the reputation is established, the photographer's services will be sought by manufacturers, food companies, restaurants, record companies, model agencies—to name only a few possible markets.

The current going rate for a point-of-purchase shot ("P.O.P.") is around $500. The day rate for some food photographers is around $1500 for the photographer and one assistant, together. Materials, travel, and specialists required for the assignment are billed in addition. Point-of-purchase photographs—those taken for displays that will confront the customer in the supermarket, salesroom, or restaurant—are very important. Pictures of food, for instance, must make the viewer want to purchase that item. The photographer who knows how to accomplish this does not have to concern himself with tie-in deals, or competitors' charges. He sets his own prices.

Pick up the classified section of your newspaper and scan it for ads placed by legal photographers. How many did you find? Legal-evidence photographers usually start in the business by writing to lawyers. They keep a low profile, and are not prominent even among members of their own local photography association(s).

Many novices start by working for an established photographer. In this way it is possible to learn the business and to see where assignments come from. This does not imply that the assistant will open a studio and try to pirate customers from his or her former associate. There is fluidity in the advertising business, and shifting of personnel and assignments is normal. Good photographers are always coming up in the ranks of commercial photography.

Merchandising of photography is basically the same as selling any other product. How you do it effectively depends both upon the product and upon the type of photography you are engaged in.

Sales—Key to Business Success

Regardless of your skill as a photographer, it is frontline sales that make you a success in the money department.

A front-line sale is the one-to-one confrontation between the customer who has the money and the vendor who has the salable product. The idea is to get the customer to purchase as many products as possible. On the other hand, the customer is seeking to get as much for the unit dollar as possible. So it is, in a way, a battle of wits. Who is going to come out on top? The photographer can always have a little edge if we remember that photography is purchased by emotion, not by logic.

Emotion, Not Logic.

Think about grandparents viewing proofs of their first grandchild's First Communion. Are they going to pass up the opportunity of purchasing a large photograph, plus several wallet-size ones? If you use the approach of the photographer who passes coupons, and photograph the entire family, will the family pass up the opportunity of having photographs of the individual children, as well as family photos for grandparents? Is a bridal album purchased upon emotion, or upon need?

The astute salesperson will utilize this emotion/logic when delivering proofs to the customer. The same technique can be used when the customer comes to the studio to pick up the final order. No photograph not included in the album should be shown to the customer unless it is framed or in a folder. Some photographers even deliver wallet photos in small folders. You enhance the product with frames and folders, and you can also increase sales by selling the frames.

Try this bit of psychological testing the next time a customer comes into your place of business to pick up an order. Have all of the out-of-album photographs mounted in frames. If the customer decides not to purchase the frames, remove the temporarily mounted photographs—and watch the expression on the customer's face. The photograph suddenly appears smaller, not as grand as when it was in the frame. Chances are very good that you will be asked to put the photographs back into the frames. Frame sales means added dollars in the till. And remember this simple fact: Most frames sell for at least double their wholesale cost. That is a nice profit for doing nothing more than stocking frames and using sales ability to move the stock.

When the framed photograph is first shown to the customer the back is secured with approximately four or six nails. It is easy to remove the picture if the customer decides not to go for the frame. On the other hand, if the sale is consumated, then the mounting is completed with additional nails. A piece of brown wrapping paper, cut larger than the rear opening of the frame, is then glued to the frame and the excess trimmed away. This hides the nails. You will see this on many expensive lithographs sold by art galleries. It enhances the product and marks it as a quality item.

Helping the Customer Helps Sales

Another sales tool is the art of friendly persuasion. Without the use of gimmicks and underhanded sales methods, the knowledgeable photographer can increase his sales when he makes up the proof albums. It is a difficult choice for many people to choose one photograph of a group and discard the others. The normal reaction is to want to keep all the photographs. How can you expect a person to choose 24 photographs out of a total of 120? How can the person make that choice if many of the shots are doubles?

The first reaction is confusion. The customer is forced to decide between duplicate shots, and then narrow down to the contracted number. "Well," you might say, "most brides buy between 40 and 50 photographs." That may be true. But you are aiming for the maximum in dollar sales, and showing duplicates is not smart salesmanship.

Most customers do not posess the discerning eye that you, a professional photographer, have. On a basis of different single photographs the choice is an easy one: How many do you want? On the basis of having to decide the best out of two, three, or four, and then culling those for the final 24, you have problems. The customer becomes thoroughly confused.

You, the photographer, can increase sales by making the initial selection for the customer. Don't present two, three, four, or more proofs of the same shot. Select *one,* and put that in front of the customer. Do this with every pose, every group, every situation, and your sales will increase. You have relieved the customer of the task of culling. The only decision the customer has is how many are wanted. If the photographer knows his business, then that decision can be a tough one. How can a bride choose 24 out of 80 excellent photographs?

The usual practice is for the studio to prepare a "presentation" album with this edited-down number of proofs, usually in 5″ × 5″ size. The customer chooses the pictures wanted for enlargement, both for the final album (which can be imprinted with the customer's name and the date or occasion) and for additional purchases. The customer feels, correctly, that each album print in "finished" size will be professionally made for him or her. Now, what about those photographs that were not selected for the final album?

When a customer sees duplicates, the first thought might be: "I'll buy those dupes for my family. They're no good to anyone else–I can get them at a good price."

That is good reverse psychology on the part of the customer. What *are* you going to do with the entire set of proofs? Let's assume that you are going to sell the proof set to the bride along with the album. With duplicates in the proof album the family will get low-cost photographs, whereas if there is only one of a kind in the proof album any additional photographs must be ordered at regular prices. That is where you make additional money.

Take the case of the photographer who makes all the "good" negatives into "one-of-a-kind" prints in 8″ × 10″ or any other size selected by the customer for the album, which he then submits to the customer for approval, in the chosen album.

The customer asks, "What happens if I choose 48 of the 100 photographs that are shown in the album?"

"We remove the photographs that you did not select and put the album together again."

"How about the ones I did not choose? What do you do with those photographs?"

"Either we keep them or we destroy them."

"In other words, the 8″ × 10″ prints that you show are really the finished photographs."

"That is correct."

"Then why destroy the ones that I do not choose? Why can't we make a deal on the entire package?"

What has happened is that the photographer's sales psychology has backfired. He expected to increase sales by using finished-size low-cost machine prints as his presentation photographs. Granted, the larger photograph carries more punch than the smaller 5″ × 5″ usually used for previews, but let's look closer.

The customer thinks: "Why should I pay $10 for each additional 8″ × 10″ print in that album when he is going to discard everything I do not choose? If I take the basic 24, then he has 76 left on his hands. Why doesn't he accept $7.50, $5.00, or even $1 for each photograph over the basic contracted amount? After all, even $76 in the till is better than 76 photographs in the trash. No wonder this photographer's prices are so high. He has to compensate for the photos he throws away. Another thing–suppose he really doesn't lose as much on the unordered photos as it appears? Then there is a discrepancy somewhere. He is probably giving me cheap 8″ × 10″ photographs to begin with."

Who is right? The customer is right! And before long word gets around about this photographer's operation. This is a negative sales approach. While it may result in increased sales for awhile, it will ultimately drive business away. The photographer will get caught in the backwash of customer disapproval.

Should Proofs Be Sold?

As long as there are two photographers remaining, the question of whether or not to sell proofs will be debated. Proofs are definitely the photographer's working tool. Some photographers realize money from the sale of proofs, while others steadfastly refuse to sell proofs under any circumstances.

The sale of proofs is a byproduct of the wedding and special-event photography business. Proofs are purchased as secondary albums for parents or grandparents, or used with other sizes of photographs to make up a mixed-size primary album. Some photographers sell proofs as primary photographs, assembling them in albums of various sizes.

What are today loosely called *proofs* are also called *previews.* They are first-run prints made from the negatives right after the film is processed. They don't fade (unlike black-and-white "sun" proofs) and, if the photographer has composed well, the results are acceptable as finished photographs. The customer doesn't care too much about perfect color balance as long as the overall tones are pleasing and there are no green flesh tones or purple cows.

Therefore, the sale (or no-sale) of proofs is really a matter between the individual photographer and the client. The term *preview* came into being when photographers wanted to get rid of the stigma of that word *proofs* because customers thought a proof was unfinished. Whatever name is used, the photographer is the one who decides what his company's method of operation will be in relation to the sale of these first-run photographs.

This brings up the subject of marking "Proof" or "Preview" on the face of the photograph. Those photographers who do not sell proofs under any circumstances do not have to concern themselves with what happens when they mark a print with that label. But there may be occasions when some type of marking may be desirable for a time, after which the marking must be removed. For that, the following information can be helpful.

While many photographers are presenting proofs, or previews, in presentation albums, others are delivering them to the customer loose in envelopes. A common practice is to mark the face of these photographs "proof" or "preview" with a rubber stamp, using a special ink for which there is a remover. Well, any photographer who marks the face of a print that may later be sold is inviting trouble. There is always the possibility that a stain may remain on the print. To one photographer who experienced this problem, the distributor of the marking product said the processing lab was at fault; the lab said the ink was at fault. Regardless of who or what was at fault, the photographer was stuck with proofs he couldn't sell because of residual stains.

Any photographer who demands white-glove handling of his negatives will never allow marking on the face of potential sales material. If you do decide to use any marking material on the face of photographs, make several tests, over a period of time, to check for stains and test the removal capability of the remover. This should be done with every bottle of the product. It is much safer, and wiser, to place all markings on the back of the photograph. You could be out-of-pocket by the amount you would have gained by selling the photographs.

Sales, Pricing, and Salesmanship

Your reputation is partly affected by the prices you charge. Anything priced consistently low carries the stigma of "cheapness." Although people do shop for bargains, they do not like "cheap" items. The term *cheap* denotes baseness in one form or another, and it can repel customers. Never tell a prospective customer, "We are cheaper than anyone else around here." It is to everyone's advantage if the customer is informed, "We have something that is *less expensive.*"

The customer may indeed purchase the "less expensive" item. Without the presence of the word "cheap" in any of your business transactions, you will not be tagged with it. "Bill's prices were less expensive," sounds better than, "Bill was cheaper than Jack."

A good sales tool in studios is the display of large-format photographs. If you show small photographs, you are going to sell small photographs. By showing the 20″ × 24″, 24″ × 30″, and 30″ × 40″ sizes, you automatically stimulate the customer into *thinking* large. Special finishes, canvas mounting, and frames are money-makers for studios. The basic expenditure for film and proof processing is the same whether the customer purchases an 8″ × 10″ or a 30″ × 40″. But the profit is much greater in the sale of the larger photograph. Keep in mind the purchase of a new car: The dealer makes his greatest profit on the accessories added to the basic automobile.

You can be the best photographer in the business, but if you are a poor salesperson you will have rough going in trying to sell your product at a fair price. On the other hand, a good salesperson can take a poor product and make the purchaser believe that it is the last of the big bargains. He can close the deal, and have the customer *thank him.*

CHAPTER 21 Collections

One of the problems in almost every business enterprise is collecting payment due on bills. With the current popularity of credit cards, most collections are problems for banks or for credit-card companies. There are, however, some collections the photographer must take care of. Bad checks will probably be with us as long as that system of exchange is in use. Our best insurance is to make certain there are sufficient funds in the payer's bank account.

Commercial accounts may present some collection problems. Some companies that pay 60, 90, or even 120 days after receiving your statement may deduct any discount shown on the invoice for "payment within X days." There are two things you can do in this instance: Insist they pay the full amount when billed, or tack on a service charge like that now used by many department stores and bank credit accounts. The company will either pay the full amount shown on the statement, on time, or drop you. It is your decision as to the amount of risk you are willing to take. A third alternative would be to call the company's local representative and have a friendly talk. You might be told payments were made from the home office on the other side of the continent, or that "the computer is down," or something else. What the double-talk means is: Either wait for your money like everyone else or forget it, we'll do business with someone else.

Factoring is another method for collecting accounts receivable. If your monthly billing is heavy and you need cash immediately, you can "sell" your receivables to a factor. You receive a percentage of the outstanding amount, and the factor collects the full amount from the clients. Factoring puts instant cash in the merchant's pocket, but the practice is not viewed favorably by the clients.

Then there are the collection agencies. Here is where you take your delinquent accounts and turn them over to the experts. If they are successful you will receive a percentage of whatever they collect. These agencies are not for your regular slow-paying accounts. They are for the ones that you have written off. If you turn a slow-paying account over to a collection agency, then you can most certainly write it off!

The truth of the matter is that Accounts Receivable provides the lifeline of the business operation. You have performed the service, delivered the product, paid your Accounts Payable–and now you need to receive your receivables.

Working with purchase orders from large companies is a sure way of knowing that the company will honor your invoices. It is simply a matter of waiting for the company to honor its obligations. Individuals usually pay in full immediately upon receiving the merchandise. If time-payments are involved, your business contract should specify the payment schedule.

Among the slowest payers, as a group, are lawyers. If you are doing legal photography, make arrangements with your clients for payment upon delivery of the photographs for each case.

Lawyers handle a great percentage of their cases on a contingency basis. That means that if they win, they get paid; if they lose, they do not get paid. The photographer cannot operate on that basis.

One attorney showed a photographer a row of files. "See all those files? There must be close to a million dollars in accident claims in them. Do you know how much I have tied up in those contingency cases? And you want me to pay you *now?*"

The photographer rose to the occasion beautifully: "Well, I'll make a deal with you. I'll wait for my money, just as you are waiting for yours. But, if you win those cases for which I have supplied photographs, then I want 40 percent right off the top as my share."

The lawyer walked over to his secretary and instructed her to issue a check for the full amount of all of the invoices.

Here, again, you are taking a chance that your client will drop you. But in the long run you will come out ahead. In the case of the irate attorney, what have you lost? Just remember that there is a vast difference between what an attorney earns from those cases and what the photographer nets from the photographs he has supplied. You cannot equate the two.

Prompt and complete collection takes perseverance and fortitude. The person in charge of this phase of the business must keep awake at all times. You cannot relax. Unless the client has a valid excuse for not being able to make the payment on time, you must keep in contact until the account is brought up to date.

Your methods of collections will differ from those of your closest friend, your associate, and even a relative in the same business. You know your clients, you know your business, and you are the one to set the policy for your collections.

The Business of Photography

CHAPTER 22

Haven't we already discussed most of what "the business of photography" is all about?

Not really. We have discussed how to organize a photographic business operation, how to set up efficiently the mechanics of the operation, the contracts, filing systems, personnel, and accounting, the role of the office manager, and other matters. But what about photography itself? For example, does the portrait photographer do nothing but portraiture? Or are there other markets for photographic specialists?

There are many ways for those in the business of photography to increase income.

There are certain times of the year when weddings are popular: the month of June and the seasons of Thanksgiving, Christmas, and Easter. The wedding photographer usually photographs bar mitzvahs, too. The bar mitzvah is a Jewish coming-of-age ceremony when boys accept adult religious responsibilities. The bat mitzvah is a similar ceremony for Jewish girls. Some of these events are not unlike weddings in the size of the receptions that follow the religious services. Like most weddings, bar and bat mitzvah celebrations are usually held on weekends.

The busy weekend photographer may do enough business to carry him through the remainder of the working week. Negatives have to be marked, proofs have to be placed in presentation albums, and finished photographs have to be inserted into albums, frames, or folders. Then there are prospective clients to talk to, supplies to be ordered, shipments to check, and myriad other things to attend to.

What Are the Risks?

There is a secret to the dividing point between a small business and a large one. If you are afraid to take the plunge and expand, then you will always remain small. If you take the challange, then you step into the major leagues of the photography business. Just as there is more money to be made behind the camera than in the darkroom, there is more money to be made behind the camera than in the menial, but necessary, accessory work. The secret to growth is to hire labor for these jobs, thus freeing yourself for the more important matters—such as making money.

Many other types of photography can provide a good supplemental income to an established business. A portrait photographer can do portfolios. But, you say, models' or actors' portfolios are appropriate for New York and Los Angeles, but not for Anytown, U.S.A. There are no movie studios here: What do you need portfolios for?

The answer is the secret of success: Innovation can pay off in dollars and cents.

Model portfolios are nothing more than a collection of photographs showing the model in various poses and lighting setups. Who says the model must be human? Can't it be a building project, say—a record of the construction. How about a collection of executive portraits? And many persons who are not Hollywood bound would like a portfolio type of portrait arrangement.

The smallest size photograph to be considered for a portfolio is 11″ × 14″, with 16″ × 20″ preferred. The 11″ × 14″ can be mounted on 16″ × 20″ board, while the larger-size photographs can be bleed-mounted (borderless).

Another item with good market possibilities is the composite, with four pictures on one side and a full-page shot on the other. Many public officials might find this type of flyer desirable, especially during campaigns. Candidates running for school, fraternity, or sorority offices might also like a composite. When it comes to the large metropolitan areas, such as New York, Chicago, and Los Angeles, model portfolios and composites are much in demand. Although many photographers in these cities specialize in portfolios and composites, there is always room for the enterprising photographer and for the one who is willing to promote this type of photography outside the modeling profession.

Researching New Markets

Food photography is another area where, if you know what should be done, you can add income to your business. There is continual need for a professional who can do the work as a fill-in. Some of the established food photographers command high prices, and there are many small restaurants and food markets that cannot afford those prices. What would you do if a small neighborhood market asked you to supply them with a few photographs for a sale? Would you tell them to call an established food photographer, or would you attempt to do the job yourself?

Knowing some of the tricks used to achieve the desired results would be the first order of business before doing the first job. Although experimenting can enlighten you to some degree, it is not the answer. A good place to begin is at seminars that are given by photography organizations, both during the year and at conventions. Talk to experts and ask questions. Read some of the publications on the subject. And *then* experiment.

Have you ever had a request to photograph a product? That opportunity comes to many portrait photographers from time to time. Although there are some tricks, and special equipment might be needed for special applications, the overall work is not too far afield from portraiture. Lighting is of prime importance, as it is in portraiture.

What about construction photography? New buildings and roads are going up all the time. Have you ever given serious thought to doing a chronological photographic report for the construction company and the owners of the structure being erected? You can never tell where this might lead. Photographs of personnel at the construction site might lead to executive portraits, stockholder reports, publications, and more. You can add to your income by expanding your frontier.

It is incorrect to assume that we can tackle any job and come away with a top-grade product. It will not happen. There are expert glass cutters who can not cut diamonds, electricians who cannot repair a television set, and carpenters who cannot build cabinets or furniture. By the like token, the photographer should not be expected to be a master of all phases of photography. Yet there are many types of photography that are similar, and experimentation can be worth while. It all depends upon the individual.

Photography is one business that has no real earnings barriers. You make your own market in photography, and you expand your business as you desire. The opportunities are present wherever you turn. It is up to the individual to set your own guidelines.

CHAPTER 23

Buying and Selling a Business

If you do not start your business from scratch you are probably going to buy one that is already in existence. Then, when you are ready to retire, or to move from that location, you will be in the market to sell your business. There are several ways in which to go about buying and selling businesses.

There are business brokers who specialize in selling. They advertise the sale, find prospective buyers, and charge a commission if the sale goes through. Some brokers help the purchaser with loan arrangements; they know the officers at local banks and can usually help smooth the way.

Many people prefer to advertise the sale themselves. The classified section of the local newspaper is a good place to start. Then there are nationally distributed professional photography magazines whose classified columns are read by persons like yourself—professional photographers. If you think you might attract a buyer from another section of your state or from another part of the country, then place notices in leading newspapers in that locality. A good example of this would be a California business offering advertised in *The New York Times.* There are people seeking to relocate, and a newspaper like *The New York Times* has a large circulation and a wide area of distribution.

Check It Out

In buying, it is best to have an accountant investigate thoroughly the business books of the studio you are considering. Accountants can generally tell when records have been "doctored." Although you may not be able to pull this off, it is a good idea to ask to see the income tax returns for the last three years. Some annual city license fees are based upon gross sales, and you should have your accountant find out what base the studio owner used in computing the taxes paid for the last three years. And if there is a sales tax in the locality, those records will also give you a good idea of how accurate the business ledger really is.

It is well known that some persons do not show all income in the open ledger. However, it is upon the open ledger that the sale is being offered, and it is the open ledger that the buyer is depending upon. It is not the intention of the author to instruct the reader how record ledgers should be maintained, in whole or in part. According to law, every business transaction must be shown in the ledger. What the individual does is his own concern. If the businessman needs capital, the banks will consider the loan on the basis of the open ledger and the income tax returns for previous years. Why should someone looking to buy the business proceed differently?

There are many items to be considered—by the seller as well as the buyer—in the purchase price of a business. Income is one of these factors. Gross income is important, but net income is more so. If the studio did a gross of $250,000, with a net after taxes, employees' salaries, utilities, rent, etc., of only $15,000, then something is definitely wrong somewhere. A return of 6 percent is not much these days, when interest rates are over the 10-percent mark. Again, this is for you and your accountant to discuss.

The remaining time on the lease is another fact to be considered. The long lease is preferable. It is not desirable to purchase a business and then have to enter lease negotiations eight months later. A two-year lease with option to renew would be a preferred minimum. As a seller, you should try to get a short lease extended or renewed prior to the sale. As a buyer, you should insist upon a long lease, as it is decidedly to your advantage. (Review the discussion of leases in Chapter 10.)

When you are paying X amount of dollars "for the key," that means you are paying for the business itself. This may—or may not—include the established name. You will have to add extra for equipment. If you are paying for the equipment as well, then find out what is included. Are cameras, lenses, tripods, backgrounds, strobes, lights, props, and darkroom equipment included? How about any stock of frames, folders, and albums? Then there are desks, chairs, typewriters, filing cabinets, and carpets to be considered. And the list goes on, and on, and on.

What the Price Includes

What does the asking price really include? That is a very important part of the transaction. Imagine that you purchase a photography business for $25,000 and then find out that it is like buying a new car. The

$25,000 is the base price and everything else is additional. You are burdened with filling up those empty premises with all that makes a business a business.

In either buying or selling a business, any outstanding debts must be made known. These debts can be in the form of unpaid invoices for materials, equipment, labor, or even chattel mortgages. (Chattel mortgages are those where a borrower offers a material item as a guarantee that the loan will be repaid.) If the purchaser will not assume the debts, then they must be paid off by the seller before the signing of the final papers, and proof of satisfaction in full presented to the purchaser. If, on the other hand, the purchaser agrees to assume any of the existing indebtedness, then that must be considered in arriving at the actual selling price.

Another important consideration is the continued use of the established name. Will the purchaser be allowed to use the name, or will a new name be required? In the case of the new name, must the change be immediate or will there be a transitional period?

There should be a provision that the seller cannot open another photography business within a specified distance or time, with or without the use of the established name. This is to protect the buyer from unethical business practices. After all, having purchased a business, the thing he or she needs least is competition from the former owner.

Another restriction should be written into the sales agreement: The former owner cannot join another studio in the area and then send notices to that effect to his former customers or advertise that fact in the news media.

If you work with your accountant and your attorney, your protection is pretty well guaranteed.

Closing Comment

The combination of an excellent photographer, excellent salesperson, and excellent business manager in one person is rare. It does happen, though, and a one-person enterprise can be operated by that sort of individual. In a large operation, authority must be delegated to others who will share in responsibility for the business. With a good working team, the result can be a successful business operation. Get your business organized, staff it with qualified personnel in the right positions, and you will see it succeed. You will have a winning combination. It all begins with effective business management.

——Sy Gutterman

Index

Accountant, 79–80, 155–157
Accounting and bookkeeping, 79–97
Accounting forms, 82–83
Additional photograph file, 50
Advertising, 136–137
  classified telephone directory, 137
  direct-mail, 140
  window, 136
  word-of-mouth, 136
  See also Sales promotion
Agreement(s)
  alternative, 14–15
Album(s)
  presentation, 43
  proof, 44, 144–148
Album tabulation form (A.T.F.), 53, 54, 55
Amateur vs. professional, 24–26, 123, 134–135
Anomalous reflectance, 17
Apprenticeships, 121
Assignment(s), 71
  contracts, 15–16, 29
Assistants, value of, 113–114

Bar/Bat mitzvahs, 152
  albums-only form, 48, 49
  information sheet, 75, 77
Billing, 149
Bookkeeping system, basic, 81
Bridal shops, 141
Business of photography, 152–154
  risks, 152
Business structure, 9–10
  basic types of, 9
Buying and selling businesses, 155–157
  debts, outstanding, 157
  established name, use of, 157
  gross income, 156
  lease, 156
  net after taxes, 156
  purchase price, 156
  restrictions, 157

Camera restriction card, 24–25, 134
Cancellation
  clause, 18
  fee, 22, 25
Car expense, 18, 87–88
Cash receipts, 81
  cumulative, 93
  sample of, 89
Caterers, and sales promotion, 137
  See also Party coordinators
Chattel mortgage, 157
Child photography, interval program, 141
Collections, 149–151
  agencies for, 149–150
  checks, bad, 149
  factoring, 149
Color film, handling, 44
Commercial account, collection from, 149
Commercial photography, 101, 141–142
Commissions to sales representatives, 137
Communications, 115–116
Competition
  amateurs, 24-25, 123, 134–135
  former owners, 157
Composites, 153
Condition-of-sale agreement, 14
Conduct, professional, 109
Construction photography, 154
Consumer advocates, 137
Contract(s)
  basic, 11–14
  cancellation clause, 18
  contingencies, 17
  how to write, 20–30
  photography business, 11–20
  for professional photographer, 20–30
  sample, 22–23
  studio, sample, 22
  suitable, 11
  terms and conditions, 12
  time charges, 17–18
Contract number, 31
Copyright, 26, 60
Corporation, 9
Costs, analysis of, 129–131
Coupon merchandising, 138–140
Customer instruction sheet, 59
Customer relations, 117–119

Damages, 12–13, 23
Darkroom. *See* Processing
Delivery date, 23, 29
Deposits, 25
Disclaimers, 14, 75

Education, 120–122
Emotion, utilization of, 143
Equipment, 123–125
  depreciation of, 124
  duplicate, 124
  maintenance of, 124
  reliability of, 124
Expenses
  car, 87–88
  overhead, 130
Exposures, too many, 133

Factoring. *See* Collections
Family, photography of, 100, 139–140
Fashion photography, 15
File card(s)
  commercial-client card, 34
  legal-client card, 35
  regular client, 33
Files, record, 35–36
Filing system, 31–37
Film filing, 44
Financial records, 155
First Communion, 143
Follow-through, 116
Food photography, 141–142, 153–154
Forms
  additional photographs, 49
  album only, 46, 49
  disclaimers, 75
  information, 75–78
  permission, 60–71
  wedding information, 75
  See also Order forms *and specific headings*
Frames, utilization of, 143–144
Freelance photographer, 105
Fringe benefits, 109–111

Gift shops, 141
Gremlins, 16
Grooming and dress, 108–109

High schools, 140
Hiring, 109, 112
Hot-stamp numbering, 41

Income, how to record, 88–91
Index, proof-negative, 38, 41, 42, 51

Individual ownership, 9
Information forms
  bar/bat mitzvah, 75, 77
  wedding, 75, 76
Inventory photography
  release agreement, 69–71

Job numbers, 31

Lab notes, 49
Lawsuits, 12–13, 62
Lawyers, collection from, 150
Layouts, sample, 57
Lease(s), 102–104
Ledger(s)
  accounts, 82, 95, 96
  accounts receivable, 81, 90
  balance sheets, 82
  coded headings, 88
  data, entering, 83–86
  disbursements, 72, 81, 85
  cumulative, 91
  monthly sums, 86
Legal photography office, 101
Legal photography release agreement, 66–69
Liability, 14–15
Location shooting, 15
Logo, studio, 59, 66

Markets, new, 153–154
Marketing. *See* Sales
Master number list, 32
Maternity shops, 141
Medical photography, 69, 113
Model portfolios, 153
Model release agreement(s), 29, 60, 62–66
  card, 64
  long form, 64
  short form, 62

Needs, determining, 82–83
Numbering
  albums, 53–56
  clients, 32–35
  consecutive, 38
  contracts, 31
  files, 31–35
  jobs, 31
  master list, 32
  negatives, 38, 39, 41, 43
  proof, 41, 43
  repetitive, 40
  successive, 38
  transparencies, 44–45

Office manager, 111–112
Order forms, 46-52
  additional photographs, 50
  albums 47, 48, 57–59
  general, 51
  See also Forms

Partnership, 9
  limited, 10
  unlimited, 10
Party coordinators, 137
Party package, photographer and, 137
Permission. *See* Releases
Personal grooming, 106, 109
Personnel, 107–114
Petty cash, 86–87
Photographer(s)
  amateur, 24, 105, 135
  freelance, 105
  hiring other, 112–114
  photojournalist, 105
  professional, 105–106
Photograph ordering instructions, 58
Photo restorations agreement, 71–75
Point-of-purchase (p.o.p.) photographs, 142
Portfolios, 153
Portrait market, 138–141
Premises and contents
  release agreement, 69
Presentation album, 43
Previews. *See* Proofs
Price factors, 131–132
Pricing, 129–132
Print index, 44
Prints, marking, 40–41
Processing lab, 126–128
  color, 126–127
  commercial, 126
  competition, 127
  personal, 126
Product and premises photography
  assignment, 71, 73
  release agreement, 71, 72
Product-liability clause, 26
Professional Photographers of America, 14, 21
Profit, 131–132
Profit picture, 133–135
Proof album(s), 43, 144–148
Proof/preview index, 42
Proofs, sale of, 43, 146–148
Purchase order (P.O.), 11
  See also Form(s); Order forms

Receptionist, 107, 116
Records, client, 37
Releases, 60–78
  inventory photography, 69–71
  legal photography, 66–69
  medical photography, 69
  minors, 61, 68
  model, 60
  product and premises photography, 71
  restorations (disclaimers), 71
  right to privacy, 61–62
Representative sampling
  of photography, 24
Restorations, 71–75
Right to privacy, 61–62

Sale(s)
  front-line, 143
  how to close, 117–118
Sales and marketing, 136–148
Sales promotion
  caterers and, 137
  coupons, 138
  flyers, 141
  party coordinators and, 137
  See also Advertising
Shopping at home, 25–26, 118–119
Signatures, 68
Snapshooter, 134
  amateurs, notice to, 24–26
Studio, 98–104
  locating, 98–99
  planning interior, 99–102
Supermarket-parking-lot distribution of flyers, 141

Taxes, 124
Telephone, 107, 116.
  manners, 115, 116
  quotations, 119
  selling by, 116
See also Communications
Transparencies, handling, 44

Weddings, 53, 113, 152
  albums-only form, 47
  information sheet, 75, 76
Witnesses, 69
Work done for hire, 68
Work Order (W.O.), 11